SELF-ESTEEM FOR TEENS

STEP-BY-STEP SELF-HELP GUIDE TO BOOST CONFIDENCE, MANAGE ANXIETY & TRAIN YOUR MINDSET

Mary Rossignol

Contents

A Note of Gratitude

I've been surrounded by giants my entire life, starting with my parents.

Dad, Peter Sr., your strength and unwavering values were a steady force in our lives. Mom, Florence "Flo," your love, faith, and the promise you made to name me Mary have constantly reminded me that I was born into purpose.

To my brothers, Rick, Peter Jr., Bob, and Jim, you didn't just protect me, you inspired me. You showed me what excellence looks like in sports, life, and character.

Pete, having you as my coach in high school was more than a privilege; it was life-shaping. You believed in me, guided me, and led by example. Watching you mentor others with humility and strength helped me discover my calling.

I carry each of you with me in everything I do. This book is as much yours as it is mine.

Introduction

Let me tell you about Noah, a high school sophomore with a talent for drawing. Despite his artistic gift, Noah was nervous to share his work. At school, he felt invisible, overshadowed by students who seemed more confident and outgoing. Even when someone saw his art, said they loved it, and tried to lift him up, He still didn't believe in himself, convinced he wasn't good enough. This constant self-doubt caused him stress and led him to withdraw from friends.

It wasn't until Noah began to understand the roots of his low self-esteem that he changed his perspective. He learned to celebrate his strengths, and slowly, he began to share his art with others. This gave him confidence, and he finally felt like he belonged.

This book aims to give teens like Noah the tools to build self-esteem, create a positive self-image, and enhance their mental strength and social skills. It is designed to guide you through strategies to help you feel more confident in your abilities and how you relate to the people in your life.

Today's teens face different and, in many ways, more intense challenges than ever. Social media can make them constantly compare themselves with others, and the pressure to succeed at school and life can be fierce. Navigating friendships can be complicated and sometimes overwhelming. According to recent studies, nearly 70% of teens report feeling stressed about schoolwork, and many teens struggle with anxiety related to social interactions and body image.

Hi, I'm Coach Mary. For over 40 years, I've poured my heart into coaching and mentoring young athletes. Whether working with boys or girls, in public schools, private academies, or club teams, I've always believed in the power of sports to shape lives. As a high school Head Girls' Basketball Coach, I've celebrated over 200 career wins and helped 26 players take their game to the college level. I've also been blessed to receive multiple awards in basketball and softball, but the real rewards have always come from watching my athletes grow.

Sports have taught me that grit, focus, and heart can transform not just games, but lives. I've seen shy kids become leaders, setbacks turn into comebacks, and young people find their confidence, one practice, one challenge, and one breakthrough at a time.

My passion for teaching life skills goes beyond the game. I've always aimed to help young people build strong self-esteem and respect for themselves and others in all areas of life. I wrote this book to give you strategies to navigate your teen years with confidence and strength.

This book is for you: teens who want to boost their self-esteem, and parents looking for ways to support your journey. Educators and counselors will also find valuable insights here. Together, we can work to sharpen the skills that will help you create the life you want with confidence.

Inside, you'll find advice designed to get you through your unique challenges. We'll explore how to understand and manage your emotions. You'll discover ways to recover from setbacks. We'll discuss the impact of social media and how to use it positively. You'll find tips on goal setting and improving your social skills, helping you build meaningful friendships.

But this book isn't just about reading; it's about doing. Try the exercises and strategies provided in each chapter to get the best results. These are proven methods to help you reach your goals. They require dedication and effort, but you'll be unstoppable if you put your mind to it. Please take this journey seriously, commit to your growth, and use this book as a tool to discover your strengths and abilities.

As you read, remember that growth takes time. It's a journey, not a race. The journey is worth taking, as the rewards of building self-esteem are lifelong. You can master the confidence you need to succeed in life and your relationships with friends, family, and everyone you meet. Take advantage of this opportunity to improve your life and become the best version of yourself.

TRUST THE PROCESS

Let's begin this journey together.

You have the power to create a more confident, thriving you.

Chapter 1

Understanding Self-Esteem

A few years ago, I coached a young athlete named Ava. She was a talented basketball player, but something was holding her back. After observing her interactions with her teammates, it became clear that Ava struggled with self-esteem. She hesitated before making decisions on the court, uncertain about her abilities.

Off the court, Ava was shy and often looked nervous, avoiding situations where she might stand out. As we worked together to build her confidence, I saw a transformation. Ava started to trust herself more, not just in sports but in all areas of her life. Understanding self-esteem was the key that unlocked her ability to excel.

What is Self-Esteem?

Self-esteem is how you see and feel about yourself. Think of it as your internal mirror, how you look at yourself in your mind's eye. It involves two main parts: self-worth and self-respect. Self-worth reflects how you value yourself, not based on what others think or say, but on what you truly believe. Self-respect is linked to how you treat yourself and expect others to treat you.

Another critical thing to consider is your internal dialogue. This is the ongoing conversation in your head, as well as thoughts and beliefs about who you are and what you can achieve. Positive self-talk can boost your self-esteem, while negative self-talk can lower it. Self-perception also plays a role; it's how you interpret your experiences and abilities. Together, these elements form the foundation of self-esteem.

Self-acceptance is crucial in this mix. It means recognizing and accepting all parts of yourself, even the ones you're not too happy about. We all have strengths and weaknesses; embracing them is essential to healthy self-esteem.

But how does self-esteem develop? It starts early in life and takes shape as you grow. Childhood experiences are key; the encouragement or criticism you receive shapes how you see yourself. Parents play a significant role in this process. Supportive parenting can lead to a strong sense of self-worth, whereas consistent negative criticism from your parents can cause it to deflate. As you age, your social environment, friends, schoolmates, and community also impact how you see yourself.

Your teenage years are especially crucial for self-esteem development. During this time, you explore your identity and figure out where you fit. Adolescence is filled with challenges and changes that can affect how you value yourself. High self-esteem during these years supports a positive outlook and improves mental health. It also fuels motivation and participation in learning and builds your emotional strength, helping you navigate stress and setbacks.

Socially, self-esteem influences your relationships and how you relate to friends and other students at school and around your community. When you value yourself, you're more likely to form healthy connections with others. A strong sense of self-worth can help you resist peer pressure and make choices which fit your values.

Now, let's talk about the difference between self-esteem and self-confidence, two concepts often confused but unique in their meanings. Self-esteem relates to how much you appreciate and value yourself and your overall worth. On the other hand, self-confidence is believing in your abilities to perform specific tasks or face challenges effectively.

While these concepts are related, they're not identical. You might feel confident about your math skills (self-confidence) but still struggle with a general sense of worth (self-esteem). The connection between the two is key; improving one can positively influence the other. Building confidence in specific areas can contribute to stronger self-esteem.

Understanding these slight but significant differences is essential for anyone looking to improve their self-esteem or support someone else in their self-esteem journey. Recognizing that both components are crucial, it's important to define clear personal growth and development strategies.

Exercise: Reflect on Your Internal Dialogue

Take a moment to consider how you talk to yourself daily. Write down common thoughts or phrases that come to mind in different situations. What kinds of words do you say to yourself? Are they primarily positive or negative? Reading what you write each day and reflecting on this can help you become more aware of your internal dialogue's impact on your self-esteem.

Self-esteem doesn't stay the same forever; it grows as you do. By encouraging positive thoughts and accepting and celebrating who you are, you can develop a healthier, stronger sense of self-worth that will help you through life's challenges and triumphs.

The Impact of Self-Esteem on Teen Life

Josh often sits in the back row of his history classroom, head down, avoiding eye contact with the teacher. He has a lot to say, as he likes to read about history in his free time and follows the lessons closely, but fear holds him back. This fear isn't about not knowing the answer; it's the fear of being wrong. That fear often stems from low self-esteem. Even when Josh is almost sure his answer is correct, he stays quiet and doesn't participate.

Self-esteem plays a vital role in a school setting. When teens believe in their worth, they tend to engage more actively in learning. They ask questions, participate in discussions, and tackle challenges head-on. On the flip side, when self-esteem is lacking, motivation tends to disappear.

Students like Josh might shy away from complicated subjects or avoid participating due to a fear of failure. This can lead to missed learning opportunities and a lack of willingness to take risks, which are necessary for growth and discovery. As a result, their grades can suffer, not because of a lack of ability but because of a lack of belief in themselves. Josh needs to choose confidence over fear.

Relationships are another area where self-esteem leaves its mark. Teens with healthy self-esteem often show strong communication skills. They're more likely to express their thoughts and feelings openly because they trust themselves and those around them. This trust leads to deeper connections with family and friends. They feel secure enough to be vulnerable, allowing friendships to grow based on genuine understanding and respect for one another.

In contrast, low self-esteem can hold teens back, making it difficult for them to open up. They may fear judgment or rejection, leading to shallow friendships that don't have much meaning. The inability to communicate effectively can result in misunderstandings and strained relationships. This can be a source of stress and conflict for families and friends, leaving teens feeling alone despite being surrounded by people.

Emotional well-being is also closely tied to self-esteem. Teens with high self-esteem often have a greater ability to regulate their emotions. They recover from setbacks more quickly because they see challenges as opportunities for growth rather than impossible obstacles. This perspective helps them manage stress effectively and develop healthy coping strategies.

In contrast, low self-esteem can lead to anxiety and depression. When teens constantly doubt their worth or abilities, it can lead to feeling hopeless or thinking they are not good enough. Minor stressful situations become overwhelming, and without the right tools to cope, these feelings can spiral into more serious mental health issues. Managing these emotions becomes complicated when teens don't believe they can change.

However, high self-esteem isn't just a shield against poor outcomes; it brings many positive benefits too. Teens with high self-esteem levels are often more resilient and open to change. They're open to new experiences because they trust their ability to handle whatever comes their way. They approach life with enthusiasm and curiosity, knowing that mistakes are part of learning and not a sign of failure. This helps them navigate life's ups and downs and brings a sense of life satisfaction and happiness. Feeling good about yourself makes you more likely to enjoy your experiences and appreciate the world around you.

Moreover, self-esteem influences how teens think about their future. Those with high self-esteem set ambitious goals and pursue them with confidence. They don't fear failure because they understand it's a stepping stone to success. This mindset increases satisfaction as they build lives that work within their values and hopes.

At its core, self-esteem is an internal compass guiding teens through the hurdles they face during these sometimes complicated years. It affects how they perform, form relationships, manage emotions, and think about their futures. Understanding its impact is crucial for anyone aiming to support young people through their teen years.

High self-esteem isn't just about feeling good; it's about empowering teens to live fully and be true to themselves. It's about helping them recognize their worth and potential so they can approach life's challenges with confidence and grace. By building healthy self-esteem, we lay the foundation for a fulfilling life marked by inner strength, happiness, and meaningful connections with others.

Common Misconceptions About Self-Esteem

Rachel is a smart, talented person who usually feels good about herself. She has positive relationships with her friends and family and enjoys participating in drama clubs and sports at school. However, she sometimes feels low and thinks negatively about herself and her performance. This frustrates Rachel, and she questions why she can't feel confident during these low times.

One of the biggest myths about self-esteem is that it should always be high. This idea often misguides many of us into believing that feeling good about ourselves every single moment of every day is the ultimate goal. However, this couldn't be further from the truth, and it is essential to bust this myth to pave a healthy path for our mental well-being.

Self-esteem is like a rollercoaster journey, with its natural ups and downs, twists and turns, highs and lows. These are natural responses to the ever-changing landscape of our lives, reflecting our human capacity for growth. Whether it's the stress of a demanding exam, moving to a new environment, or the complexities of a new friendship, these experiences naturally influence our inner thoughts about ourselves.

It's perfectly normal for self-esteem to go up and down with these challenges. This dynamic process doesn't portray instability but reflects our remarkable ability to navigate and grow through varying circumstances and environments.

A persistent myth exists that self-esteem means using willpower to convince yourself of your worth. While personal reflection and inner dialogue are important, influences from others and the world around you have a mighty impact.

For instance, comparing yourself to others can cause a lot of external pressure. In today's digital age, social media platforms such as Instagram and TikTok swarm users with images of what appear to be picture-perfect lives. The filtered and often unrealistic versions of what you see can lead you to compare yourself to fake versions of reality.

Additionally, the way your family interacts can heavily influence self-esteem. Parents' or guardians' expectations and the cultural practices and values in the home environment can powerfully shape individuals' perceptions of their worth and identity. Understanding how your family interactions influence your views of yourself allows for more insightful approaches to tackling your self-esteem.

Another common belief is that self-esteem is a fixed trait set in stone from birth. Yet, this couldn't be more inaccurate. Self-esteem is as workable as clay and can change and develop over time. Engaging in personal development and taking time to understand and embrace personal strengths and weaknesses can shed new light on self-perception.

Participating in therapy or peer support groups can provide spaces where such growth is encouraged. Within these settings, individuals can find tools and techniques for overcoming negative self-perceptions, thus enhancing their self-worth. Acknowledging the potential for change and progression means accepting that we're all works in progress and that our journey of self-discovery and self-improvement is continuous.

Furthermore, many mistake high self-esteem for cocky, incorrectly assuming self-love means you think you're better than others. However, healthy self-esteem is about valuing your own unique attributes without putting others down. Having a positive sense of self-respect without crossing into the territory of overconfidence is possible.

Overconfidence tends to involve an exaggerated perception of one's abilities, which might lead to reckless behavior by ignoring potential consequences. In contrast, healthy self-esteem is firmly grounded and recognizes strengths and limitations, thus enabling more reflective and balanced decision-making.

To paint a clearer picture, think of a scenario in which a teenager steps boldly onto the stage for a play. They feel a bundle of nerves, yet they give off a calm confidence that comes from being prepared and naturally talented.

This is not arrogance; it is confidence nurtured by dedication and self-belief. Even if a line slips from their mind during the play, perfection does not define their self-worth. Instead, healthy self-esteem lets them receive praise gracefully without letting their egos swell. It's all about finding the right balance.

False beliefs like these can cloud how we see ourselves and hold us back from growing. But when we understand that self-esteem can change, recognize how outside things affect us, and learn the difference between real confidence and arrogance, everything starts to make more sense. With that clarity, it's easier to accept the ups and downs of self-worth as a natural part of life and to use those moments to grow, reflect, and learn.

Self-esteem misunderstandings can lead to disappointment, yet they don't have to confine or restrict one's growth. By challenging these myths, we can build an environment where true growth can happen. Where life's ups and downs are not merely accepted but anticipated as an important part of its lively and varied nature.

Identifying Your Current Self-Esteem Level

In understanding self-esteem, it's vital to recognize where you currently stand. This isn't about labeling yourself but rather gaining clarity about your self-perception. One effective way to discover this is through self-assessment tools and exercises. Journaling, for instance, is a simple yet powerful method. Grab a notebook and spend a few moments each evening reflecting on your day. Write down situations that made you feel good about yourself and those that didn't. Over time, as you read your thoughts back to yourself, patterns emerge, providing insights into your self-esteem.

Another tool is self-esteem questionnaires or quizzes. These structured assessments can offer a snapshot of how you perceive your worth. Such quizzes often include statements like "I am satisfied with myself" or "I feel I have much to be proud of," asking you to rate how true these feel to you. The goal isn't to score high or low but to pinpoint areas where you need more support or reflection.

Recognizing signs of low self-esteem can also be enlightening. Many struggle with negative self-talk, frequently beating themselves up for perceived shortcomings. This constant stream of self-doubt often leads to avoidance behaviors such as steering clear of social situations for fear of judgment or failure. Suppose you notice a pattern of negative results on self-esteem quizzes or find yourself withdrawing from activities you once enjoyed. This may indicate that your self-esteem needs some work.

To begin boosting your baseline self-esteem, start small. Set achievable goals that you can realistically meet. These don't need to be huge; even simple tasks like organizing your study space or completing a hobby project can offer a sense of accomplishment. Success in these areas can slowly build confidence, making bigger challenges more approachable.

Incorporating gratitude and positive affirmations into your daily routine can also help. Begin each day by listing three things you're grateful for or repeat affirmations like "I am capable" and "I am worthy" to reinforce positive thinking. Over time, these practices can shift your mindset from self-criticism to self-compassion.

Feedback from trusted sources is another valuable tool in understanding and improving self-esteem. Conversations with mentors, coaches, or counselors can provide external perspectives highlighting strengths you might overlook. These individuals often offer constructive feedback based on their observations, helping you see yourself through kinder eyes.

Peer feedback also plays a role in this process. Friends who genuinely care about your well-being can offer insights into how they perceive your strengths and your positive actions. They can provide reassurance and encouragement when you're feeling uncertain about yourself.

Exercise: Self-Esteem Reflection

Take a few minutes to write down a recent experience where you felt challenged or unsure of yourself. Reflect on what happened, how you responded, and what you learned from the situation. Discuss this experience with a trusted friend or mentor to gain more perspective.

Improving self-esteem isn't an overnight task; it requires patience and persistence. But every step you take to understand your current level and work toward enhancing it is a victory in itself. You hold a wealth of potential within you, waiting to be acknowledged and celebrated. As you continue on this path, embrace your progress and the person you are becoming. Your worth isn't defined by others but by the value you see in yourself.

As we go through this book, remember that self-esteem is a lifelong companion in your personal growth story. By nurturing it, you're building a stronger sense of self and paving the way for richer experiences and deeper connections with those around you. The journey may not always be smooth, but determination and support can lead to massive transformation and fulfillment.

Chapter 2

Embracing Authenticity

The Power of Authenticity

Jordan is at a party. His favorite music is playing, and he's surrounded by friends chatting and laughing. Though he's close to those around him, he feels like an outsider. Everyone seems to fit a mold, but he can't shake the feeling that he is playing a part. Have you ever felt that way? It's exhausting.

Here's the thing: being true to yourself can change everything. When you embrace who you are, something magical happens. Stop worrying about meeting everyone else's expectations and live according to your values. Being authentic sets you free.. It frees you from the stress of trying to fit in and allows you to pursue genuine happiness and fulfillment.

Living authentically means aligning your actions with your beliefs. It means being the same person in any room and not changing yourself to suit different situations. When you're true to yourself, you're happier because you're not wasting energy pretending to be someone you're not. You find satisfaction in your relationships because they're based on honesty.

Imagine how much simpler life would be if you didn't feel pressured to conform to others' expectations. Authenticity reduces the stress of constantly adjusting your behavior to fit others' standards, freeing you to be your true self.

Society doesn't always make it easy to be authentic. Everywhere you look, there are pressures to conform, from social media influencers showcasing perfect lifestyles to peer groups with specific norms. The world tells you what you should wear, how you should act, and even what you should think.

Social media can be particularly challenging, as it often presents idealized versions of life that can make anyone feel inadequate (Child Mind Institute, n.d.). It's easy to fall into the trap of comparison, constantly measuring your worth against these unrealistic portrayals. But remember, these are just snapshots, not the whole picture.

Peer pressure is another hurdle many face. The desire to belong is powerful, and sometimes it feels like the only way to gain acceptance is to fit into a box (KidsHealth, n.d.). However, sacrificing being yourself for acceptance can lead to internal conflict. Your relationships become shallow and unsatisfying when you pretend to be someone you're not. Instead of connecting with people who appreciate you for who you truly are, you're stuck maintaining an image that eventually becomes tiring.

The long-term benefits of authenticity are many. When you're genuine, you attract others who value your true self, leading to deep and meaningful relationships. These connections are based on trust and mutual understanding because everyone can be open about who they are. Living authentically aligns your career path with your values and passions, resulting in greater job satisfaction and success. When your career reflects your true self, work becomes more than just a paycheck; it becomes a source of pride.

So, how do you build authenticity in a world that often encourages fitting in? Start by reflecting on what truly matters to you. Ask yourself what values guide your decisions and what passions light up your soul. One practical exercise is journaling about moments when you felt most yourself versus when you didn't (Randy Taran, n.d.). Read what you write often and honestly think about your own words. Doing this can reveal patterns and help identify areas where you're not being true to yourself.

Another method is practicing self-compassion. Accept that you're a work in progress and that flaws are okay. Embrace your unique qualities instead of hiding them. Surround yourself with supportive people who encourage your authenticity rather than try to change you into someone you're not. Seek out environments where you can express yourself without fear of judgment.

Exercise: Discovering Your Authentic Self

Take a moment to list three values that are important to you. Then, write about an experience where living by these values made you feel fulfilled or happy. Reflect on how these moments align with your authentic self.

Consider setting boundaries that protect your authenticity. Learn to say no when something doesn't align with who you are or what you believe in. This might mean stepping away from relationships or situations that require you to compromise your values.

Remember, embracing authenticity is not about being perfect; it's about being real. It's about showing up as yourself, flaws and all, and finding joy in who you genuinely are. The journey toward authenticity may not always be easy, but it's one of the most rewarding paths.

Navigating Identity Challenges

Adolescence is a whirlwind of discovery. You're figuring out who you are, your beliefs, and how you fit into this complex world. One of teens' most significant challenges is understanding their identity amidst all this change. Cultural identity can be a tough one. You might find yourself balancing the expectations of your cultural heritage with your desires. It can feel like you're living two lives, one at home, where traditions are upheld, and another with friends, where different norms apply. This balancing act can be difficult, leaving you wondering where you truly belong.

Personal values are the principles that guide your decisions and behavior. Defining these values can be tricky, especially when they conflict with what others expect of you. These conflicts can affect your sense of self, whether it's the pressure to conform to standards or the desire to live up to family expectations.

Self-exploration is key to getting through these challenges. Journaling is an excellent tool for this. Set aside a few minutes daily to jot down your thoughts and feelings. Ask yourself questions like, "What do I value most in life?" or "How do I feel about my cultural background?" This practice encourages reflection and helps clarify your thoughts. Identity exploration workshops and online resources can also be valuable. These spaces offer opportunities to engage with others on similar paths, providing support and new perspectives.

Community plays a vital role in shaping your identity. Being part of a supportive group can make a difference when trying to understand yourself better. Consider joining sports, clubs, or support groups that align with your interests or identity. These communities offer a sense of belonging and acceptance, helping you feel more secure in who you are. Seeking mentorship from trusted adults or friends can also provide guidance and reassurance during times of uncertainty.

Of course, conflicts between different aspects of your identity are bound to arise. You may be torn between wanting to fit in with friends and staying true to your cultural roots. These conflicts can feel overwhelming, but there are strategies to help manage them. Learning conflict resolution skills is essential. This means developing the ability to communicate your feelings effectively and finding compromises when needed.

One approach is practicing empathy, trying to understand the perspectives of those who may not see things as you do. It's not about agreeing with them but understanding their viewpoint while staying true to yourself. Another strategy is setting boundaries that protect your identity. This might involve honest conversations with friends or family about what's important to you and why.

Remember, navigating identity challenges is an ongoing process that requires patience and self-compassion. There will be times when things feel clear and other times when everything seems confusing. The important thing is to keep exploring and questioning until you find what works for you.

Reflection Section: Identity Discovery

Think about a time when you felt conflicted about your identity. Write about what happened, how it made you think, and what you learned from the experience. Consider sharing your thoughts with someone you trust to get a fresh perspective.

Identity is like a puzzle of many pieces, each representing a different part of who you are. Some pieces fit together easily, while others have to find their place. Allow yourself the grace to explore each one without pressure or judgment.

In this journey of self-discovery, celebrate your uniqueness and embrace the diversity within you. You are not alone in this process; countless others are walking similar paths, each with their own stories and struggles. Together, through understanding and support, we can overcome these challenges and grow into the individuals we're meant to be.

Setting Boundaries to Protect Personal Identity

Joan's family just moved to a new city, and it is her first week at a new school where she doesn't know anyone. She just met a girl named Candace, who seemed welcoming at first. However, the more time she spends with Candace, the more Candace teases her for her love of reading. Joan doesn't like how

Candace treats her, but she has no other friends, so she stays silent and keeps hanging out with her.

If you've ever experienced something similar, you know how hard it can be to stand up for yourself. In situations like these, gaining a sense of your own boundaries is crucial. If Joan had strong boundaries, she would talk to Candace, and if Candace didn't change, she would not tolerate her behavior and reach out to make other friends instead. Imagine having a personal bubble that shields your true self from outside influences. That's what setting boundaries is all about. It's like drawing a line in the sand that says, "This is who I am, and I'm not going to let anyone change that." Setting boundaries means deciding what you will and won't accept in your life, from how others treat you to how much time you spend on activities that matter to you. It's about recognizing your worth and protecting your identity from being overshadowed.

When you establish these boundaries, you create space for your authentic self to shine, free from the expectations of others. This is crucial in a world that often tells you who you should be instead of celebrating who you are.

Exploring your creativity is another powerful way to express your identity. Think of hobbies and interests as windows into your soul, offering glimpses of the real you. Whether it's painting, playing an instrument, or hitting the basketball court, these activities allow you to express yourself in ways that words sometimes can't.

Engaging in the arts, music, or sports showcases your talents. It helps you discover hidden abilities you might not have known existed. Trying new activities can lead to unexpected passions, opening new doors for self-expression. These creative activities become a form of communication, a way to share your unique perspective.

Creative expression offers significant mental and emotional benefits. It acts as a way to release pent-up emotions, reducing anxiety and providing a sense of calm. When you're deeply involved in a creative task, worries disappear, replaced by a focused sense of purpose. This process can boost your self-esteem as you see your own growth and achievements.

Creating something beautiful or meaningful enhances your confidence, reinforcing the belief that you are capable and talented. Each completed project is a testament to your abilities, helping you build a stronger self-worth and feel more confident in all you can do.

There are countless forms of self-expression to explore. Fashion and personal style are powerful ways to communicate who you are without saying a word. Your clothing choices can reflect your personality, mood, and the things you enjoy. Similarly, digital platforms offer opportunities to share your creative work with a wider audience.

Whether posting photography on Instagram or sharing writing on a blog, these platforms allow you to connect with others who appreciate and support your expression. The digital world becomes a gallery where you can show your individuality and receive encouragement for further exploration.

Celebrating unique qualities is about recognizing and sharing what makes you memorable with the world. Everyone has a story worth telling, filled with experiences that have shaped who they are today. Sharing these personal stories can be empowering, creating connections with others who relate to your journey.

Participating in cultural, religious, or community events is another way to celebrate your uniqueness. These events often highlight diversity and encourage individuals to embrace their heritage and personal stories. By participating, you're celebrating yourself and contributing to a tapestry of diverse voices and experiences.

Reflection Section: Celebrating Your Uniqueness

Take a moment to write down three qualities or talents that make you unique. Reflect on how these traits have shaped your life experiences and how they contribute to your identity.

Ultimately, embracing your individuality is about recognizing that being different is not only okay but something to celebrate. The world is richer for its diversity of perspectives, and your unique contributions add depth and color to it all. By setting boundaries, exploring creative ways to express yourself, and celebrating what makes you unique, you're not just protecting your identity but allowing it to shine brightly for all to see.

Building A Personal Brand

Imagine your personal brand as your very own signature. It's how you present yourself to the world and can shape how people see you personally and remarkably. A personal brand reflects your values, skills, and passions. It makes you stand out, like a beacon in a sea of sameness.

In today's digital age, your social media presence plays a huge role in building this brand. Every post, comment, or shared article contributes to the picture others see of you. It's like leaving digital footprints everywhere you go, and you want them to reflect who you are.

Aligning your personal brand with your goals is also crucial. Think about what you want to achieve after you graduate and how your current actions and online presence support that vision. For instance, sharing sustainability-related articles or projects can reinforce your brand. This prepares you for future opportunities and helps connect you with like-minded people and potential mentors in your field.

Consider what truly matters to you to identify your core values and strengths. What are the principles that drive your decisions? What activities make you lose track of time because you enjoy them so much? Value identification exercises can be beneficial here. Try listing five things you believe in passionately. Then think about times when you felt proud of yourself – what were you doing? These moments can highlight your strengths.

Strengths assessment tools can also offer a good look into what you excel at. Whether it's problem-solving, creativity, or empathy, understanding these strengths allows you to build a brand that genuinely represents who you are. Embrace these qualities as they are your unique points.

Communicating your personal brand becomes the next step once you've identified your core values and strengths. Crafting a personal mission statement can be a powerful tool. This statement should summarize who you are and what you aim to achieve. Keep it simple and straightforward, something which can guide your actions and decisions. A strong mission statement provides clarity not just for others but also for yourself.

Developing a consistent online presence is equally important. This means making sure that your social media profiles align with your personal brand. Consistency in tone, content, and imagery helps solidify your brand's image.

A strong personal brand opens doors to numerous opportunities. When people understand who you are and what you stand for, they will remember you when opportunities arise. Whether it's internships, scholarships, or job offers, a well-defined personal brand can make all the difference. It acts like a magnet, attracting opportunities that align with who you are and what you want.

Building a personal brand is more than just creating an online persona; it's about understanding yourself deeply and sharing that understanding with the world. It's an ongoing process that evolves as you grow and change. By aligning your online presence with your core values and long-term goals, you're setting yourself up for success in both personal and professional areas.

As we wrap up this chapter on authenticity and identity, remember that being true to yourself is the foundation of everything we've discussed. From setting personal boundaries to building an impactful brand, authenticity remains at the heart of it all. It empowers you to navigate life's challenges with confidence and clarity. As we move into the next chapter on resilience, consider how authenticity strengthens your ability to overcome obstacles and thrive in adversity.

Chapter 3

Building Resilience

Peter is on the track team, and he really loves to run. He wins a lot of races, and his record is outstanding. However, he is nervous about a big meet coming up, and even though he practices, his times aren't as good as he wants them to be. When the meet arrives, he feels a lot of pressure to win, which only aggravates his nerves.

Peter runs great times in most of his races, but doesn't place in the 100-meter race. He is devastated and angry at himself and even considers quitting. The pressure he puts on himself gets to him, and he's lost as to where to go from here. What Peter lacks in this moment is a healthy sense of resilience.

Understanding Resilience

Picture yourself as a rubber band. You stretch, bend, maybe even twist under pressure, but you never entirely break. That's resilience. It's the remarkable capability to recover from difficulties, adapt to change, and maintain strength through life's ups and downs.

Far from just a buzzword, resilience is an important skill for personal growth and development. It provides the strength necessary to rebound from setbacks, whether on a challenging exam that didn't go well, a race you lost, or a friendship that ended, allowing you to come out of these experiences more assertive and more self-aware.

Resilience is about bouncing back and is vital to mental health and well-being. When you are resilient, coping with stress, managing anxiety, and tackling everyday challenges become more manageable tasks. It's like having a mental toolkit that aids you in remaining calm and focused, even when you are down and things look hopeless.

According to the University of Queensland (n.d.), resilience doesn't mean avoiding challenges; instead, it's about confronting them with confidence, knowing that you can navigate them, even though it may be difficult.

Resilience involves a relationship between emotional regulation and mental flexibility. Emotional regulation effectively manages your emotions, ensuring they do not overshadow your rational thoughts and actions.

Imagine being caught in a heated argument. Instead of letting impulsive reactions take over by lashing out or shutting down, emotional regulation guides you to pause momentarily, followed by deep breaths. This helps you respond thoughtfully and in a way that helps the situation. Techniques like deep breathing exercises or practicing mindfulness are key in achieving this balanced state of emotional control.

Cognitive flexibility, on the other hand, refers to adapting your thinking to accommodate new challenges. It's like possessing a multi-purpose tool, enabling you to switch strategies and approaches when confronted with problems. This adaptability significantly helps with overcoming obstacles and creating solutions. For instance, if your plan A ends up being a bust, sensible flexibility empowers you to pivot seamlessly to plan B without feelings of defeat or disappointment getting the better of you.

Moreover, resilient individuals commonly show specific traits that enable them to navigate life's hurdles with remarkable grace. One such trait is optimism, the capability to keep a positive outlook even when things seem challenging. This doesn't mean ignoring problems; instead, it's about believing that positive outcomes are possible.

Problem-solving skills further underscore the nature of resilience. Resilient individuals are resourceful, think on their feet, and are unafraid to reach out for assistance when necessary, embracing collaboration rather than isolation.

Cultivating resilience has an array of benefits that have the potential to transform your life. For starters, it enhances your confidence in managing future challenges. Knowing you've overcome hurdles can empower you to face new ones head-on. Additionally, you'll likely discover that resilience improves your relationships. By mastering emotional management, you keep calm, cool, and collected, thus reducing the likelihood of reacting impulsively or letting stress strain your connections with others.

Reflection Section: Discovering Your Resilience

Please take a moment to think about a time when you faced a challenging situation and consider how you managed it. What did you learn about your personal ability to cope? Write down the strategies you used and reflect on how they might help you with similar challenges in the future.

Building resilience is more than just survival; it's about thriving in adversity. It involves taking lessons from every experience and learning the strength to confront whatever comes next with courage and determination. As we get further into this chapter, remember that resilience isn't something everyone is born with; it's a skill anyone can grow with practice if you don't give up. Through patience and applying yourself, resilience evolves into a defining aspect of your character, fully equipping you to embrace the unpredictable journey of life with steadfast determination and genuine optimism.

Learning from Setbacks

Imagine standing at the base of a mountain, looking up at the peak surrounded by mist. Every path seems steep, and every rock is a potential stumbling block. Life often mirrors this scene; setbacks are those rocks and steep trails. Yet, what if we viewed these obstacles not as barriers but as stepping stones to higher ground?

Reframing setbacks as opportunities for growth can transform challenges into powerful learning experiences. It's all about perspective. When faced with a setback, consider what can be learned from the situation instead of dwelling on failure. This approach shifts your inner dialogue from a fixed mindset, where abilities are seen as unchangeable, to a growth mindset, where every challenge is an opportunity to develop new skills and learn about yourself.

One effective method of overcoming setbacks is through reflection. By analyzing past challenges, you uncover patterns and lessons you might have missed in the moment. Journaling can be a great tool here. Writing down your experiences allows you to process emotions and reflect on what went wrong and why. It's like a conversation with yourself, where you can explore your thoughts and feelings without judgment.

Additionally, talking to friends, family, teachers, and coaches can provide fresh perspectives. Others might see solutions or lessons you hadn't considered and offer valuable advice on tackling similar situations in the future.

Problem-solving techniques can also play a big role in overcoming obstacles. These methods help break down seemingly impossible challenges into manageable parts. Start by identifying the root causes of your setbacks. Ask yourself: What led to this situation? What types of things contributed? Once you pinpoint these causes, you can develop an action plan to deal with them. This might involve setting specific goals or seeking advice from those who have faced similar issues. A clear plan provides direction and purpose, making it easier to move forward confidently.

Persistence and perseverance are key when dealing with adversity. Feeling defeated after a setback is easy, but maintaining effort over time is essential for progress. Setting small, step-by-step goals can help you keep up your motivation. Break down your goals into smaller, achievable steps instead of focusing only on the result.

Celebrate each small victory along the way, as these successes build momentum and encourage continued effort. Remember, progress isn't always noticeable; there will be ups and downs, but each step forward reinforces your determination and resilience.

When you encounter setbacks, recognize them as part of life's learning curve rather than as failures. Embrace them as moments of growth and self-discovery that shape who you are becoming. Even if the path seems overwhelming, remember that every experience, whether triumphant or challenging, contributes to your personal development. As you continue climbing your mountain, know that each step brings you closer to reaching new heights of understanding and strength.

In this way, setbacks become more than just challenges; they are opportunities for transformation and growth. By approaching them with curiosity and determination, you unlock potential within yourself that you might not have known existed. With each obstacle overcome, you gain confidence in your ability to handle whatever comes next, ready to face new challenges with courage.

So next time you face a setback, pause and reflect on what it might teach you. Consider how you can grow from the experience and use it as a stepping stone toward greater resilience and self-awareness. Remember, you're not alone in this journey; countless others have faced similar challenges and emerged stronger. By learning from setbacks, you equip yourself with the tools to navigate life's ups and downs gracefully and confidently.

Keep pushing forward, knowing that every step you take brings you closer to realizing your full potential. As you build resilience through these experiences, you'll find that the peaks once surrounded by mist are easier to see, revealing new paths and possibilities waiting to be explored.

Darla has just joined her soccer club team. Though she's been playing since she was little, she finds that many other players on the team are much more advanced than she is. At first, she is discouraged, but she sets her mind to improving her skills. She practices hard every day and scores two goals in the team's first game. Darla's mental toughness allowed her to work hard, rise to the occasion, and excel at the sport she loves.

Developing Mental Toughness

Consider mental toughness as your mind's personal trainer, conditioning you to stay strong and focused even when life throws curveballs. It's maintaining concentration and keeping cool, especially under pressure. This mental stamina helps you manage stress without crumbling.

Imagine you're in a difficult situation, like a big exam or a competitive game. Your heart races, and your mind starts to wander. Mental toughness steps in here, allowing you to channel that energy into focus. It's like having tunnel vision that blocks out distractions and keeps you on track toward your goal.

Emotional resilience is another critical piece of mental toughness. You can control emotions, even when they threaten to spiral out of control. Picture yourself facing criticism or dealing with unexpected setbacks. Instead of reacting impulsively, emotional resilience allows you to pause, process, and respond thoughtfully.

It's about not letting emotions decide your actions, but instead using them as information to make better decisions. This ability to regulate emotions keeps you grounded and enables you to bounce back from challenges with renewed energy.

Building mental strength isn't just about understanding these concepts; it requires active practice. Visualization techniques are a great starting point. Please close your eyes and imagine yourself in challenging scenarios, visualizing success in overcoming them. For instance, picture yourself acing that presentation or confidently handling a difficult conversation. This mental rehearsal prepares your mind for real-life situations, making them feel more familiar and less frightening when they occur.

Another effective exercise is controlled exposure to things that cause stress. Gradually let yourself get used to situations that trigger stress in a manageable way. Start small; it could be speaking up in a group discussion or tackling a difficult task. As you get used to handling these stressors, your endurance increases, and you become better at managing stress.

Self-discipline plays a huge role in developing mental toughness. The inner drive keeps you committed to your goals, even when your motivation is low. Daily routines can help you grow this discipline. Make yourself a schedule that includes time for work, rest, and self-care. This structure organizes your day and reinforces habits that support your mental well-being.

Over time, these routines become second nature, making it easier to stay disciplined even when life gets hectic. Identifying what motivates you is equally important. What drives you? Is it the desire for personal growth, following a passion, or the satisfaction of achieving a goal? Understanding what motivates you empowers you to tap into that energy whenever challenges arise.

Sustaining mental toughness is an ongoing process that requires regular attention. Conducting mental health check-ins is one way to maintain resilience over time. Set aside moments each week to reflect on your mental state. Ask yourself how you feel, what challenges you've faced, and what strategies you have used to manage stress effectively. These self-assessments help you identify areas for improvement and make sure you're taking active steps to support your mental health.

Mindfulness practices are another valuable tool for enhancing focus and resilience. Engage in meditation or deep breathing exercises that center your mind and body. These practices cultivate awareness and help you stay in the present moment without worrying about the past or the future, allowing you to approach challenges with clarity and calm.

Exercises such as yoga or tai chi can enhance mental toughness by promoting physical and mental balance. These practices teach patience and persistence, helping you develop a resilient mindset that embraces challenges as opportunities for growth.

Ultimately, developing mental toughness equips you with the skills and mindset needed to face life's challenges head-on. It's about building a solid foundation of focus, emotional resilience, self-discipline, and motivation that empowers you to navigate conflict confidently and gracefully. By committing to these practices, you're not just strengthening your mind but empowering yourself to thrive in any life situation.

Inspirational Stories of Perseverance

Let me tell you about a few people who have faced serious hurdles and kept going. Take an athlete who tears a muscle mid-season, with dreams of championship glory seemingly gone. Instead of surrendering to defeat, they commit to intense rehabilitation, fueled by a strong belief in their return to peak performance. They ignore the odds and clinch victory the following season through grit and determination.

Such stories shed light on the resilience that drives individuals beyond physical limits, reinforcing that the mind can often overpower the body when determination takes the lead. This is true in life as well as in sports.

In the business world, consider someone who faces rejection after rejection while trying to pitch a groundbreaking idea. Imagine the frustration and doubt creeping in with each "no." Yet, it's their adaptability and persistence that eventually lead to success. They tweak their approach and learn from each setback.

These tales of determination reveal that failure isn't an endpoint but a stepping stone toward success. The path may be rocky, but those who keep going often find themselves at the front and center of groundbreaking achievements.

What can we learn from these stories? First, they emphasize the importance of persistence. It's tempting to give up when things get hard, but if you keep going, you'll often find something great waiting for you on the other side. Adaptability is another key takeaway. Situations change, and being able to adjust your approach is important for success.

These stories also highlight the valuable role of support systems, family, friends, or mentors who provide encouragement and guidance during tough times. Knowing you aren't alone can make all the difference.

To truly benefit from these lessons, find role models who demonstrate resilience. You don't have to look far; resilient people are everywhere. Start by researching individuals you admire. Dive into their stories to understand how they navigated challenges and emerged stronger.

Engaging with mentors who have faced adversity can offer real-life insights and advice specific to your situation. These connections give you a front-row seat to resilience in action, showing that even giants in their fields started somewhere small.

But here's where it gets personal: your story matters, too. Sharing your experiences with others empowers you and can inspire those around you. Reflect on your moments of resilience and when you faced challenges head-on and emerged stronger. Communicate these stories with friends or write them down in a journal to read to yourself when you're feeling down. Sharing your journey helps you process experiences, recognize growth, and build confidence.

As we wrap up this chapter on resilience, remember that setbacks are not barriers but opportunities for growth. Each challenge you face is a chance to learn something new about yourself, to adapt and evolve. The stories of others remind us that we are all capable of extraordinary things when we refuse to give up. As we move forward, think about how these lessons can apply to your life and how you can continue to build resilience as you face adversity.

The next chapter will focus on strengthening social skills, an essential aspect of building and maintaining relationships that support resilience and personal growth. By enhancing these skills, you'll find it easier to connect with others, seek support when needed, and create a network that uplifts you in times of need.

Chapter 4

Handling Criticism and Peer Pressure

Differentiating Between Criticism and Feedback

Imagine yourself in an art class, a calm place where creativity knows no bounds. You've just taken the daring leap to display your latest masterpiece. The quiet buzz of the classroom hums in your ears as anticipation mixes with anxiety.

A classmate walks over, curiosity in their eyes. They glance at your canvas, pause, and say, 'The colors don't go together.' Just like that. It's blunt and cold, like someone opened a window and let the chill in on a warm day.

You feel the sting, it hits like a splash of cold water you didn't see coming. But before the moment sinks too deep, your teacher steps in with a warm smile. 'I see what you're going for,' they say, their voice calm and supportive. 'Try blending the colors a bit more to make the contrast pop.' That's what real feedback sounds like—honest, helpful, and meant to help you grow.

The difference between criticism and feedback is rooted in the feeling and intention behind the message. Blunt, harsh criticism tends to spotlight faults and gaps without any positivity involved. It is much like telling someone a painting is crooked without suggesting they straighten it.

On the other hand, feedback is meant to be helpful. It provides a guide to assist you with improvement. When someone comments about your work, reflect on the comments and pinpoint whether they originate from a place of kindness or from somewhere negative, bitter, or jealous.

Engaging with feedback can be likened to unwrapping a present. When feedback is presented, accept it with grace and gratitude. This approach highlights your openness and maturity. Expressing appreciation ensures that those around you are more inclined to share their perspectives in the future.

Accepting constructive feedback can help you along your path to personal development. To best utilize positive feedback, take what is said and channel it into your goals if it is helpful. For example, your teacher, aware of the possibilities for you to improve your writing, recommends developing clarity in your essays. Let this advice help you with future assignments. A journal can help you keep track of constructive criticism, and ways you can use it to improve..

Reflection Section: Transforming Feedback into Growth

Reflect on a recent time when you received feedback. Explore your initial emotional response. Was it surprise, defensiveness, or perhaps a mix of emotions? Each reaction offers insight into areas you may wish to improve. Write down what you learned from the feedback, including ways to incorporate those lessons.

Both criticism and feedback can function as mechanisms for self-improvement. When you can tell the difference between the two and are open-minded, they can help you grow.

Building Confidence to Resist Peer Pressure

Peer pressure is an invisible force that nudges you to act in ways you might not choose. It can make you worry about what's cool or obvious, with friends daring you to participate in activities that don't sit right with you. Understanding peer pressure is vital for learning how to handle it.

Direct peer pressure is straightforward. You might hear, "Come on, just try it," or "Everyone's doing it," pushing you toward immediate decisions you're uncomfortable with. Indirect pressure is more about implied norms. It's the unspoken expectation to conform to a group's behavior just to fit in. This kind of pressure can lead you to second-guess your choices, making it challenging to stand up for yourself.

So, how do you hold your ground when faced with these pressures? It starts with assertive communication. Practicing how to say "no" confidently can be empowering. It's not just about saying no; it's about doing so with clarity and conviction. Try rehearsing scenarios where you might face pressure, like turning down an invitation to a party where you know there will be things you're uncomfortable with.

Role-playing with a friend can help. It allows you to experiment with different ways to express your decision without feeling guilty or awkward. This builds a muscle memory of confidence, making real-life situations easier to handle.

Self-awareness plays a massive role in resisting peer pressure. Your internal compass keeps you aligned with what truly matters to you. When you understand your core values, those non-negotiable beliefs that define who you are, making decisions that honor them becomes more manageable.

Reflecting on personal goals is equally important; they guide your actions toward what you want to achieve. Regularly reminding yourself of these values and goals reinforces your ability to resist influences that steer you off course.

Building a supportive network is another effective strategy. Surround yourself with friends who respect your boundaries and share similar values. Joining clubs or teams where you all share mutual interests can lead to friendships based on genuine connections rather than shallow ones. These relationships can provide encouragement when facing challenging situations. Seek out friends who celebrate your individuality rather than trying to mold you into someone you're not.

Imagine having friends who cheer you on for being yourself, who see the real you, and encourage you instead of pressuring you into uncomfortable situations. They're out there, and finding them might take some effort, but it's worth it. These friendships contribute significantly to self-esteem and confidence, serving as reminders that it's okay to stand out and stay true to yourself.

Remember you're not alone when you're in environments with intense peer pressure. Many face similar challenges, and seeking advice from trusted mentors can provide additional support and perspective. They can offer strategies based on experience, helping you navigate complex social situations more easily.

As you build these skills and relationships, resisting peer pressure will come more naturally. Your confidence in making decisions that reflect your true self will grow, transforming interactions with others from stressful tests into opportunities for genuine connection and growth.

Maintaining Self-Worth in the Face of Criticism

Imagine for a moment the effort and dedication you put into a project, only to be met with an unexpected critical comment or gesture that makes you doubt your work. Such a situation can be jarring to your senses. Criticism can profoundly affect your mental and emotional well-being, especially when it arrives in a harsh manner or when you least expect it.

It has a way of creeping into your inner thoughts, instigating self-doubt. It can initiate a relentless cycle where you question your abilities and doubt yourself. Over time, this can erode your self-confidence. The fear of facing further judgment may make you reluctant to express your creativity. If left unchecked, this may lead to a distorted view of yourself.

If this happens, one highly effective strategy involves reframing negative feedback, viewing it as an opportunity for growth instead of a personal insult. By consciously altering your perspective, you can transform criticism into a tool for self-betterment. This process involves examining the criticism to identify underlying patterns or areas that you can use to enhance your skills or understanding.

Reframing criticism encourages emotional detachment, enabling you to analyze the feedback objectively and constructively. Additionally, actively focusing on your past achievements and strengths can offer a grounding effect against negativity. Take time to remember your successes, big or small, and celebrate the qualities that make you unique. Maintaining a journal to record accomplishments or positive feedback can help reinforce your self-worth and remind you of your capabilities.

Building resilience in the face of criticism is important to maintaining emotional well-being and mental health. Mindfulness practices can offer great tools in developing this resilience. Techniques such as deep breathing or mindful meditation teach you to be present in the moment, which can help prevent criticism from getting to you.

These practices can help you to respond thoughtfully and deliberately rather than react impulsively to criticism. Additionally, a routine centered on positive self-affirmations strengthens your resilience. Begin each day by reminding your self of your value and potential with statements like "I am capable" or "I am constantly growing and changing for the better." Such affirmations help you build a supportive internal dialogue that boosts your self-esteem and acts as a protective barrier against negativity from others.

Seeking support from trusted people is essential in maintaining your emotional strength. Opening up to friends, family, or mentors provides reassurance, guiding you through constructively processing criticism. Choose to confide in those who offer honest yet positive feedback. Participating in support groups provides a similar place where you can share experiences and find mutual encouragement, helping you feel validated, understood, and connected.

By weaving these strategies into your daily routine, you can build a resilient foundation of self-worth that stands against the impact of criticism. Looking at criticism positively, staying focused on what you're good at, practicing mindfulness, and leaning on people you trust all work together to help you build strong self-esteem. This approach transforms criticism from a potential source of insecurity into a powerful tool for growth, equipping you with the confidence and clarity needed to face challenges head-on.

Navigating Social Media Influences

Social media is like a busy city square, with voices and images all competing for attention. It's a place where everyone seems to be living their best life, but this can be misleading. The online photos are often carefully curated to showcase only the highlights. People post their best moments, the vacation sunsets, the perfectly plated meal, the flawless selfie after countless tries.

This selective sharing creates a warped reality that can make you feel like you're not good enough. You might compare your everyday life to these idealized images and feel you don't measure up. This can lead to a distorted self-image and pressure to conform to these artificial standards.

The trick to handling social media's influence is using it on your terms. Start by curating your online feed to reflect positivity and inspiration. Follow accounts that uplift you, whether they share art, motivational quotes, or stories of personal growth. Be mindful of the content you consume and how it makes you feel. If certain accounts trigger negative emotions, don't hesitate to mute or unfollow them. Remember, you have control over what you see.

Not everything you read or see online is trustworthy or reliable. Develop a critical eye by evaluating sources before accepting information as fact. Consider who created the content and for what purpose. Are they experts in their field or sharing personal opinions without evidence?

Additionally, be aware that algorithms influence what appears in your feed. These algorithms prioritize content based on your past behavior, potentially creating an echo chamber. Recognizing this can help you seek different perspectives and avoid getting trapped in a bubble of similar ideas.

Setting boundaries with social media is another essential step to maintaining your well-being. It's easy to lose track of time while scrolling through endless feeds, but setting screen time limits can help prevent overuse. Decide how much time you're comfortable spending on social media each day and stick to it. Create digital detox routines where you disconnect from screens entirely, allowing time for real-world connections and activities that bring you joy.

Consider adding activities like reading, exercising, or spending time outdoors into your routine during these breaks. These moments away from screens offer a chance to recharge and refocus, reducing the feeling of being overwhelmed by the digital world.

As we wrap up this chapter on handling criticism and peer pressure, remember that how you engage with social media is as important as what you consume. By curating a positive feed, checking your facts and sources, and setting healthy boundaries, you can navigate social media's influence without losing sight of who you are.

Social media is a powerful tool that can connect you with others and provide inspiration when used mindfully. It's about finding balance and enjoying the benefits without letting it decide your self-worth or decisions. With these strategies, you can confidently face social media's challenges and maintain a strong sense of self.

In the next chapter, we'll explore strategies for improving emotional intelligence, an essential skill for navigating relationships and understanding your emotions and those of others. This journey will further help you build stronger connections and deepen your understanding of yourself and those around you.

Chapter 5

Dealing with Peer and Family Dynamics

Decoding Family Dynamics

Imagine a classic family dinner table scene. A lovingly prepared meal fills the air with its delicious smell. The table holds not just plates and food but the hopes, histories, and feelings of everyone at the table. Family members gather, each bringing their unique flavor to the conversation. Or, the silence is more telling than words, as each person processes their thoughts.

Every family member plays a role that significantly influences how you view yourself and the world around you. These roles guide interactions and shape your mindset. Parents, siblings, and extended family help mold your self-perception.

You might find yourself distinguished as the "responsible one," the "peacemaker," or potentially the "rebel." These roles come with silent expectations that shape how you behave at home and in social settings. While these roles may occur naturally within families, they also have the potential to restrain you.

Furthermore, the attitudes projected by parents can fundamentally impact your self-esteem and confidence. Parents who offer educational support, validate your feelings, and applaud your accomplishments can help build your confidence, urging you to reach your full potential. On the other hand, parents who habitually criticize or emotionally withdraw can unintentionally lead you to feel self-doubt and insecurity.

Family compositions can shape emotional growth in varied ways. Traditional families, characterized by two parents and their children, deliver a particular type of interaction and role distribution. Meanwhile, single-parent families, blended families, and extended setups involving grandparents or other relatives each present unique challenges alongside their benefits.

For instance, children in single-parent families might develop a sense of independence at an early age due to taking on additional household responsibilities. In their combination of differing traditions and lifestyles, blended families necessitate adaptability and openness. Cultural distinctions further add layers to family interactions, with varying value systems impacting how family members connect and support one another.

Family support plays a critical role in emotional well-being. Homes that foster an atmosphere of acceptance and encouragement act as safe places for emotional expression, sharing personal stories, and seeking mentorship. Receiving emotional validation from family strengthens your sense of resilience. When families participate in shared experiences, whether through a weekly game night or strolling together in a park, these interactions build connections and cherished memories.

It's essential to acknowledge that family relationships naturally encounter challenges. Rivalry among siblings is a common issue that can lead to jealousy or competitive tension. It's common to compare yourself with siblings, yet uncontrolled rivalry risks diminishing self-worth.

Generational gaps are another common source of stress, as mismatched values, technology applications, and lived experiences between parents and teenagers can spark miscommunication and conflict. However, these obstacles present opportunities for growth and empathy, and bring families closer together when handled with care.

Reflection Section: Mapping Your Family Influence

Take some time to think about who significantly influences the familial dynamics in your home. What unique expectations do you feel rest on your shoulders? Consider how these expectations shape your actions and inner self-image. Consider talking about this with a family member; getting their perspectives might deepen your understanding. Understanding your family's impact on your identity is important to your personal evolution and empowerment.

Communicating with Family Effectively

Communication in the family can feel like a dance, sometimes smooth, sometimes awkward, and always requiring rhythm and understanding. To make this dance work, each person must practice active listening. It's about more than just hearing words; it's about tuning in to the emotions behind those words.

For example, listen to your mom's words, tone, and expressions when she talks about her day. Show empathy by nodding, making eye contact, and responding with understanding comments like, "That sounds tough," or "I can see why that made you happy." Doing so makes your mom feel heard and valued, creating a space where honest dialogue can flow freely.

Expressing your feelings with clarity is equally important. Here is where "I-statements" come into play. Instead of saying, "You never listen to me," try framing it as "I feel ignored when others don't listen." This approach reduces defensiveness and opens the door to understanding. It's a way of owning your emotions without casting blame on others, leading to a sense of openness and respect.

When it comes to setting boundaries within the family, clarity is essential. Imagine boundaries as invisible fences that protect your well-being. Communicate your limits calmly and assertively. If you need space after school to unwind before discussing your day, express that clearly: "I need a little time to relax before I talk about my day." Respecting others' boundaries is just as important. If a sibling asks for privacy, honor that request without question. Boundary-setting is a two-way street built on mutual respect and understanding.

Family conflicts are a part of life, but don't have to be destructive. Collaborative problem-solving offers a pathway to resolution. Think of it as a team effort where everyone's voice matters. Gather the family and brainstorm possible solutions to disagreements, valuing each person's perspective. This collective approach builds cooperation and strengthens family bonds. Holding family meetings can provide a safe space for discussing concerns and celebrating achievements, reinforcing unity and connection.

Shared family traditions offer another powerful way to strengthen bonds. For example, if your family enjoys cooking together, turn it into a weekly ritual where everyone contributes their favorite dish. Celebrating cultural or religious traditions helps build a sense of belonging and identity within the family.

Interactive Element: Family Communication Check-In

Choose a quiet evening to sit down with your family for a communication check-in. Take turns sharing one thing you appreciate about each family member and one area in which you'd like more understanding or support. Use "I-statements" to express your feelings clearly. Listen actively to each other, offering empathy and encouragement.

These practices create a nurturing environment where family members feel valued and supported. Enhancing communication skills, establishing healthy boundaries, resolving conflicts constructively, and building positive traditions can help families navigate challenges smoothly. Strengthening these relationships improves individual self-esteem and increases the strength of the family as a whole.

Through effective communication and meaningful interactions, families can create an environment where everyone feels respected, understood, and cherished. The journey toward stronger family connections is ongoing but rewarding, offering countless opportunities for growth, laughter, and love.

Handling Toxic Relationships

Susan and Rebecca have been friends since they were little. Though they have a lot of good times together, Susan secretly feels uncomfortable with how Rebecca pushes her around. Rebecca often makes fun of Susan and sometimes intimidates her into doing only what she wants to do, even things Susan is scared of or doesn't like. After hanging out with Rebecca, Susan often feels emotionally tired and unsure of herself.

Have you ever had a friendship that feels more draining than fulfilling? Such relationships can be confusing, as there may be moments of kindness. Yet, underneath lurks a pattern of manipulation or control, where one person consistently overpowers another.

You might notice frequent feelings of anxiety or sadness in these interactions, like a cloud that refuses to lift. Recognizing these red flags is the first step in understanding toxic relationships.

Toxic relationships can significantly impact self-esteem. Imagine carrying a heavy backpack filled with self-doubt and insecurity, weighing down your every step. Constant exposure to negativity can lower your confidence, making you question your worth. These relationships can cause emotional exhaustion and burnout, and drain your energy and enthusiasm. It's like trying to fill a leaking bucket; no matter how much you pour in, it never seems enough.

To get your power back in these types of interactions, establish clear boundaries, defining what behavior you will accept and what crosses the line. Communicate these limits assertively, ensuring they are respected. It isn't about building walls but about protecting your well-being. Seek support from trusted adults or professionals who can offer guidance and perspective. They can provide strategies specific to your situation, helping you regain control and confidence.

Sometimes, letting go of relationships that cause more harm than good becomes necessary for personal growth. Doing so can be challenging, especially when emotions are involved. However, distancing yourself from toxic interactions allows you to reclaim your emotional space.

It's about prioritizing self-care and healing, focusing on activities that bring you joy. Engage in hobbies or spend time with supportive friends who uplift you. These positive influences can remind you of what healthy relationships should feel like: mutually supportive and empowering.

As you distance yourself from toxic influences, notice the change in your emotions. You start to feel lighter and more in tune with your true self. This process is not about forgetting the past but learning from it and understanding what patterns to avoid in future relationships.

Recognizing that you deserve relationships that uplift rather than drain you is crucial. Surround yourself with people who inspire growth, challenge you positively, and celebrate your successes. Healthy connections are a two-way street, built on trust and mutual respect. They encourage you to be the best version of yourself without fear of judgment or manipulation.

The journey toward healthier relationships involves self-reflection and action. Reflect on what you've learned from past experiences and use those insights to make future choices. Be patient with yourself; change takes time and effort, but the effects can be enormously rewarding.

In this chapter, we've explored toxic relationships and their impact on self-esteem. We've discussed strategies for managing these dynamics and emphasized the importance of letting go for the benefit of your personal growth. Remember, you can choose friendships where you can thrive emotionally and mentally.

As you move forward, keep these insights close at hand. Use them as tools to navigate your present and future relationships with confidence and wisdom. The path may not always be smooth, but with determination and support, you'll find yourself surrounded by people who benefit your life in meaningful ways. Your journey toward healthier connections begins with recognizing your self-worth and embracing the love and respect you deserve.

Building Lifelong Support Systems

Imagine facing a challenge alone; it's overwhelming. Now, picture having a supportive network around you, people who lift you when times get tough. It's not just about having friends; it's about creating a circle of trust. These connections help you tackle life's ups and downs with resilience and confidence. Shared experiences with others who understand your journey can be grounding, offering a sense of belonging that bolsters self-esteem. When supportive individuals surround you, you're more likely to take healthy risks and pursue your goals because you know someone has your back.

Growing your social circle can seem intimidating, but it's filled with opportunities to connect. Joining clubs or sports teams is a fantastic way to meet people who share your interests. Imagine the bond formed over scoring that winning basket or collaborating on a project in a club meeting.

Community groups offer a great way to connect. Think about volunteering for a cause you're passionate about; it gives back to the community and introduces you to like-minded people. These shared experiences create lasting friendships built on mutual respect and understanding.

Having mentors and role models can be a game-changer. They offer guidance, wisdom, and insights drawn from their own experiences. Teachers and coaches often make excellent mentors because they see potential in you that you might miss. Their encouragement can be the push needed to overcome obstacles.

Role models inspire by example, showing what's possible when you diligently pursue your dreams. Learning from those who've walked similar paths can help you navigate your journey confidently.

Fostering diverse relationships is equally important. Imagine a world where everyone thinks and acts alike. Boring, right? A varied circle of friends brings fresh perspectives and insights. Diverse friendships help you see things differently, think deeper, and understand people from different backgrounds. Being inclusive helps you grow and stay open-minded in a world that's constantly changing.

Remember to check in regularly with friends and mentors and show genuine interest in their lives. Celebrate achievements together, offer support during tough times, and be there for them in moments of need. These small gestures strengthen bonds, ensuring your support system remains strong and reliable over time.

Reflection Section: Mapping Your Support Network

Take a moment to reflect on who makes up your current support system. List the people who provide emotional or practical support on a regular basis. Consider areas where your circle might be lacking and ways to expand it. Reach out to someone new this week, whether it's through joining a club, volunteering, or asking for guidance.

As we close this chapter on building support systems, remember that you are never truly alone. There are countless opportunities to connect with others who understand and appreciate you for who you are. With each relationship formed or strengthened comes growth for everyone involved.

In our next chapter, we will explore strategies for developing emotional intelligence, an essential skill for navigating relationships with empathy and understanding while building communication skills across all areas of life. As we continue this journey together, keep these insights close at hand as tools for creating meaningful connections that last a lifetime.

Make a Difference with Your Review

Unlock the Power of Generosity

> *"You don't have to do big things to make a big difference. Even small kindness counts."*
>
> — Coach Mary

Hey there, friend!

If you've made it this far in the book, that means you're already doing something amazing—you're learning to believe in yourself and grow your confidence. And that's something to celebrate! 🎉

Now, I'd love to ask you a quick favor. It's super easy, takes just a minute, and helps someone else who's walking the same path you're on.

Would you help someone just like you—maybe a teen feeling unsure, or a parent looking for answers—by leaving a review of this book?

Why does your review matter?

Most people choose books based on what others say. Your words might be the reason someone picks up this book and says, *"I can do this."*

Just imagine your review helping:

- One more teen believes in their self-worth.
- One more parent guides their child with love and strength.
- One more mentor recommends a book that really works.
- One more kid feels like they're not alone.

Your voice matters.

Leaving a review doesn't cost anything but can mean everything to someone else.

⚪ Click or scan the link below to leave a review on Amazon:

👉 https://www.amazon.com/review/review-your-purchases/?asin=B0F9XHRBB9

Thank you from the bottom of my heart for being part of this journey. If you believe in lifting others up, you're already making the world a better place.

With gratitude and hope,

Coach Mary Rossignol

"Start right here, one page at a time."

Chapter 6

Learning from Setbacks

Turning Failures into Opportunities

Picture this: you've just tried out for the school play, the biggest production of the year. You've poured hours into practicing your lines, picturing your moment in the spotlight, costume and all, with eager anticipation building inside you. Then, boom, you don't get the part.

Be a problem solver

It stings, right? It feels like a gut punch, leaving disappointment swirling around you. But imagine if instead of viewing this as a dead end, you saw this experience as just a detour, a pivot on the path to something better. You pick yourself up, knowing you can try again next year. You resolve to practice reading more plays out loud in order to prepare. You could sign up for an acting class to improve your skills.

This is the magic of rethinking failures into learning experiences and growth opportunities. When you accept setbacks as stepping stones on your life's journey, they transform from barriers into bridges that lead to progress.

Consider Thomas Edison, a great example of persistence through failure. He reportedly engaged in countless attempts to design the light bulb. Each unsuccessful effort was not merely a failure but a pivotal learning moment, and eventually, his hard work paid off.

Similarly, acclaimed author J.K. Rowling met her fair share of rejections before a publisher took a chance on the now-iconic Harry Potter series. Imagine a world where they had given up. Rather than being discouraged, these setbacks fueled their determination to refine their approach, ultimately leading them to remarkable success.

To condition yourself to practice this empowering mindset, reflect on a time when you encountered a significant setback. Write down your thoughts about the experience and go deeper than just surface-level reflections. What inner truths did this reveal to you? Which capabilities did these difficult times help you uncover or enhance? Such lessons hold a great deal of value and can serve to guide you in your future pursuits.

Undeniably, setbacks can often pack an emotional punch, arriving alongside disappointment, frustration, and lingering self-doubt. It's crucial to acknowledge these emotions rather than suppress them. The healthy processing of disappointment begins by allowing yourself the grace to feel what you are feeling. It's entirely reasonable to be upset or frustrated.

Once you've recognized your emotions, seek to channel them productively. Physical activities like exercise can provide a healthy outlet for releasing pent-up energy; a brisk walk through nature or a quick workout can uplift your spirit. Journaling your thoughts and feelings can offer profound insights. Write freely about your experience and your emotional response. Explore your emotions and any underlying fears or concerns lingering beneath the surface.

Building resilience in the face of failure is like developing mental muscles, growing more with each challenging encounter. It's about rebounding stronger after every fall. For example, athletes often face numerous defeats in sports before reaching victory.

Imagine a basketball player who misses crucial shots. It can be discouraging, but embracing adversity instead of giving up, they use those moments as motivation to practice with purpose, sharpening their skills and determination. Similarly, students may struggle with complex subjects but gradually move toward mastery by developing new learning strategies. This resilience goes beyond short-term challenges; it strengthens character and builds a foundation for long-term success.

In the world of work, resilience can lead to career advancement by demonstrating to employers your capacity to embrace challenges head-on without folding under pressure. Developing this resilience ensures you're more inclined to take on risks and seize opportunities that others might refuse.

What's the next step after encountering setbacks? Crafting a personal action plan is essential for regaining your stride. Start by figuring out what went wrong and understanding why it happened. Next, think about and write down actionable steps to effectively confront similar challenges in the future.

Set small, attainable goals to rebuild confidence and progressively monitor your achievements. Using visualization techniques can also prove beneficial. Picture yourself succeeding despite past failures, immerse yourself fully in the emotions of triumph, visualize every detail, and let this positive energy fuel your determination.

Reflection Exercise: Transforming Setbacks

Take a quiet moment to reflect on a recent setback, write down the events, the emotions involved, and the lessons you learned. Then, write yourself an action plan with steps to address similar challenges in the future with clarity and confidence.

It's important to remember that setbacks are not impossible roadblocks but temporary hurdles that can give you a moment to pause, reflect, and re-emerge stronger. Embrace them as precious opportunities for self-discovery and growth. With each challenge you overcome, you build your experience, equipping you to confidently face whatever lies ahead.

Developing a Growth Mindset: Embracing Challenges

Larry dreams of becoming a professional swimmer. He takes swimming lessons during the summer and wants to join his school's swim team. However, he's scared that he'll never make it. His self-doubt makes him question whether he can even get on the team, let alone succeed at the professional level. His negative thoughts overcome him, so he decides not even to try.

Let's discuss something that can change how you approach life's hurdles: the growth mindset. A growth mindset involves believing that effort and dedication will develop abilities and intelligence. It's like having a personal cheerleader inside your head, constantly reminding you that you can improve.

When you adopt this mindset, resilience becomes your ally, helping you handle setbacks with grace and determination. It contrasts sharply with a fixed mindset, where people see their talents as set in stone. Those with a closed-off mindset might shy away from challenges, fearing that failure could uncover what they think of as their weaknesses. But with a growth mindset, challenges aren't threats; they're opportunities to expand your skills and knowledge.

Having a growth mindset brings benefits to various areas of your life. In school, it encourages taking on new subjects without fear of failure, knowing that effort will lead to improvement. In friendships, it's essential to recognize that skills such as empathy and communication don't just come naturally; they are learned, applied, and mastered over time.

Even in your personal life, a growth mindset encourages exploration and creativity, pushing you to try new hobbies or sports without the fear of not being perfect from the start. This mindset transforms how you see success, not as a final destination but as an ongoing process of learning and growth with positive self-talk.

Developing a growth mindset requires shifting how you think about challenges and setbacks. Start by reframing negative thoughts. Instead of saying, "I can't do this," try telling yourself, "I can't do this yet." That one little word, "yet," leaves room for growth.

Replace self-defeating thoughts with positive affirmations that focus on your potential for improvement. Encourage curiosity by asking questions and seeking new experiences that push your boundaries. When you approach life with curiosity, learning becomes an exciting adventure rather than an overwhelming task.

Effort and persistence form the backbone of a growth mindset. Hard work isn't just a way to get things done; it's a path to self-discovery and improvement. Think about famous figures like Maya Angelou or Elon Musk, who didn't achieve success overnight. They faced setbacks but continued to work hard, turning challenges into opportunities for growth and eventually finding success through persistence. Their stories remind us that talent is essential, but perseverance drives lasting achievement.

Consider Thomas Edison's words: "Genius is one percent inspiration and ninety-nine percent perspiration." This saying reminds us that dedication and effort are crucial ingredients in the recipe for success. Embrace this concept by setting small goals that keep you motivated. Celebrate small victories along the way to maintain momentum and build confidence in your ability to achieve larger ones.

Engage in activities to shift your perspective and reinforce a growth mindset. Use growth mindset reflection sheets to track your thoughts and progress over time. Reflect on past experiences where you embraced challenges or learned from mistakes, noting how these moments contributed to your personal development.

Create a challenge journal where you keep track of new experiences and the insights gained from them. This practice reinforces the growth mindset and helps you recognize patterns in your responses to challenges and ways to improve on them.

Remember, developing a growth mindset is a continuous journey of personal evolution. It's about embracing the idea that every challenge you face, whether academic, athletic, or social, is an opportunity for growth. Adopting this mindset will make you more open to new experiences and more resilient in adversity.

The Power of Perseverance: Staying the Course

Perseverance is like the secret sauce that turns dreams into reality. It keeps you going when the going gets tough, like a stubborn engine that refuses to quit, no matter how steep the hill. Consider the story of Malala Yousafzai, who faced unimaginable adversity yet continued her fight for girls' education worldwide. Her perseverance was about enduring hardship and maintaining focus and commitment to her cause.

History is filled with stories of those who persisted against the odds. Thomas Edison's relentless pursuit of innovation and Rosa Parks' quiet yet powerful stand for civil rights show how perseverance can lead to monumental breakthroughs. These examples remind us that the road to success isn't always smooth, but staying the course is often rewarded with transformative results.

Yet, maintaining that perseverance can be challenging. Life throws bad passes, and it's easy to feel like giving up when faced with setbacks. Common roadblocks include self-doubt, exhaustion, and external pressures that can seem too difficult to face. You might question your abilities or wonder if it's all worth it.

These challenges are real and can make staying committed hard. But recognizing these hurdles is the first step in overcoming them. By identifying what holds you back, you can start to find ways around or through these obstacles. Whether it's a lack of motivation or fear of failure, understanding your barriers allows you to tackle them head-on.

So, how do you keep going when the going gets tough? One strategy is to set step-by-step goals. Break your journey into smaller, manageable parts instead of focusing only on the result. Celebrate each small victory along the way; it's like giving yourself a little pat on the back for progress. It keeps the momentum going and also boosts morale.

Moreover, engaging with mentors and role models can provide emotional support, help in setting achievable goals, and offer constructive feedback, all of which are essential components for growth and success. Their presence can inspire you to overcome challenges and strive for excellence in your endeavors.

A long-term perspective is crucial for perseverance. It's easy to get bogged down in day-to-day struggles and lose sight of more significant goals. Creating a vision board can be a powerful way to keep yourself on the path of future success. Fill it with images and words that represent what you hope to achieve. Place it somewhere visible as a daily reminder of why you're pushing through challenges. Aligning daily actions with long-term goals helps maintain focus and drive. Each small action becomes part of the journey and larger puzzle, fitting together to create the life you want.

Exercises like writing down your goals and reflecting on your motivations provide clarity and reinforce commitment. Ask yourself what you're working toward and why it matters. Keep these notes handy to read to yourself during tough times as a source of motivation and direction.

Perseverance requires more than willpower; it's about creating an environment where your efforts can thrive. Surround yourself with supportive people who encourage you and remind you of your strengths. Embrace challenges as opportunities to grow rather than threats to your progress.

Remember, perseverance isn't about ignoring difficulties but confronting them with resilience and determination. It's about believing in yourself and your goals, even when they seem distant or hidden. By staying the course, you're working toward success, building character, and finding a sense of purpose beyond any achievement.

As you continue on this path, remember that perseverance is a skill that grows with practice and patience. Each step forward, no matter how small, is a testament to your dedication and strength. Keep your eyes on the horizon and trust in your ability to navigate whatever challenges come your way.

Assembling a Resilience Toolkit

Imagine having a toolbox at your side, filled with everything you need to tackle life's unexpected challenges, a personalized collection of strategies, resources, and support systems designed to help you bounce back when life throws you a curveball.

It's not a one-size-fits-all solution but a custom set of tools that evolves with you. Consider it your go-to guide for managing life's ups and downs. Whether you're dealing with stress from school, conflicts with friends, or personal setbacks, this toolkit provides guidance and support when needed.

At the heart of a resilience toolkit are coping strategies and support systems. Coping strategies are like nuts and bolts, helping you manage stress and keep a balanced perspective. Deep breathing, progressive muscle relaxation, or mindfulness exercises can be beneficial. They calm your mind and body, providing peace among the chaos.

Support systems, on the other hand, are the sturdy framework that holds everything together. This includes family, friends, teammates, mentors, or anyone who provides encouragement and understanding. Building these connections ensures you have people to turn to when things get tough.

You'll want to include specific tools and resources to enhance resilience further. Stress management techniques are crucial; they help you deal with anxiety and prevent it from overwhelming you. Try creating a relaxation routine, a daily walk, a yoga session, or quiet time with a favorite book. Join clubs, teams, or groups where you can meet people with similar interests or seek out communities focused on personal growth. These connections can offer valuable insights and encouragement, making it easier to navigate challenges.

Personalizing your resilience toolkit is key to making it truly effective. Everyone's needs are different, so your toolkit should reflect what works best for you. Start by customizing it with personal affirmations and goals that match your values. Positive affirmations can boost confidence and remind you of your strengths during difficult times.

Adding hobbies and interests to your toolkit as resilience boosters can also be incredibly helpful. Engaging in activities you love can lift your spirits and provide a sense of achievement, contributing to your overall well-being.

Resilience plays a significant role in maintaining mental and emotional health. A well-developed toolkit helps you navigate stress more effectively, reducing its impact on your life. Regularly updating and revisiting your toolkit ensures it remains relevant to your evolving needs.

Consider setting aside time each month to reflect on what has worked well and what might need adjustment. Exercises like journaling about recent challenges or setting new goals as needed can provide clarity and direction, keeping your toolkit updated.

Reflection Exercise: Personalizing Your Resilience Toolkit

Take a few moments to think about the tools that help you feel strong and supported. List coping strategies that work for you and any support systems for which you're grateful. Consider how you can personalize these things to suit your unique needs better.

As we wrap up this chapter on learning from setbacks, remember that resilience isn't about avoiding difficulties but facing them head-on with courage and creativity. By assembling a resilience toolkit tailored to your needs, you're equipping yourself with the resources to thrive despite adversity. This toolkit becomes a shield against life's challenges and a map guiding you toward personal growth and self-discovery.

Our next chapter will explore how emotional intelligence can enhance your ability to connect with others and understand yourself more deeply. This journey into emotional awareness will complement your resilience toolkit, deepening your capacity for empathy and strengthening relationships along the way.

Chapter 7

Healthy Coping Mechanisms

Stephanie puts a lot of pressure on herself to do well in school. She's intelligent and studies hard, but when it comes time to give a presentation or take a test, her stress becomes so intense that it feels like it's eating her alive. Because she doesn't have the right coping mechanisms to deal with her stress, she often freezes up at test time, leading to lower grades. She knows she can do better, but doesn't know how to overcome the stress.

Understanding Stress and Its Impact

Stress can be similar to a surprise quiz. It can seem to appear out of nowhere, and can make the challenges of life seem impossibly large.

At its core, stress is your body's adaptive response to demands or hurdles. It has a dual nature and can serve as a motivator, nudging you to sharpen your studying efforts or push your limits in a race. However, it becomes problematic when it lingers, developing into persistent stress and significantly impacting well-being.

Stress can stem from academic pressures, particularly for teenagers who feel like every test or project is under relentless scrutiny. The pressure to succeed and excel can make school seem like an arena where each task is a defining battle. Each assignment looms large, feeling as critical as any life-changing decision.

Beyond academics and sports, social surroundings introduce another dimension to stress. The complex mix of friendships, friend groups, and social circles can feel like walking a tightrope, it can be a delicate balancing act. In this environment, one misstep might feel like the ground disappearing beneath you.

Furthermore, family expectations form a substantial piece of the puzzle. These expectations often concern academic grades, sports, behaviors, and future goals, casting long shadows over individual creativity and the pursuit of personal interests.

When stress is present, the body reacts in many different ways, some of which are not openly visible but have significant impacts. The physical response includes a faster heart rate and tense muscles, while the mind races with negative or anxiety-inducing thoughts.

It's like being constantly stationed on high alert; every minor incident feels magnified. As a result, concentrating on even the simplest tasks becomes overwhelming, and irritability increases, turning minor inconveniences into significant challenges.

Stress can wear not only on your physical body but also your mental health; it eats away at self-esteem, sowing seeds of doubt about future successes, which grow into significant fears of failure. As these doubts increase, confidence can decrease, often leaving individuals hesitant to pursue challenges. This avoidance repeats a cycle of skipped opportunities, leading to regret and, sometimes, a reduced sense of self-worth.

Acknowledging and recognizing stress is the first step in managing it effectively. A helpful method is maintaining a stress diary. Writing down stressful moments helps identify triggers and patterns, revealing trends that can be anticipated and managed when similar stressful situations come up again.

Another way to navigate stress is through mindful daily check-ins. Regularly pausing to assess your emotional state can help a lot. Ask yourself if your heart is racing or if you're experiencing physical tension; these signs indicate that stress levels may be rising.

Reflection Section: Stress Awareness Exercise

Carve out time every evening to think about your day. Write down three times when stress crept in and consider what was at the heart of those moments. Was it tied to academic challenges, social interactions, or other concerns?

Engaging in this reflection not only aids in pinpointing sources of stress but also shows patterns in how you react. If you write down and analyze these patterns over weeks and months, trends become evident, enabling you to effectively develop tailored strategies to manage these stress-inducing situations.

As this chapter progresses into more coping methods, it's vital to remember that stress, while undeniably a part of life, does not define who you are. By acknowledging and understanding the forces of stress, you're already on your way toward utilizing them effectively. This awareness is essential to developing resilience and creating room for personal growth, transforming stress from an adversary into a manageable challenge met with confidence.

Relaxation Techniques for Teens

Imagine this: you've just finished a long, intense game, and your mind is buzzing with deadlines, group projects, and commitments. Your heart feels like it's racing in a marathon. What if you could train your body to enter a calm, restful state, counteracting the stress that seems to cling to you? Understanding the relaxation response can be a huge ally.

The relaxation response is your body's way to unwind, a remedy to stress that invites peace and tranquility. It's like flipping a switch in your nervous system. These are the ones that tell your heart to slow down and your muscles to loosen. It's about promoting a state of ease, making space for calm.

Deep breathing exercises are one of the simplest ways to spark this relaxation. You may think breathing is something you do automatically, but there's a technique to draw the most benefit from it. Diaphragmatic breathing involves taking slow, deep breaths from your diaphragm, not just your chest. Imagine filling your belly like a balloon as you inhale deeply through your nose, holding for a count of four, then slowly exhaling through your mouth. This technique helps reduce tension and brings immediate relief.

Another way to chill out fast is the 4-7-8 breathing trick. Breathe in through your nose for 4 seconds, hold it for 7 seconds, and slowly let it out through your mouth for 8 seconds.

This simple rhythm helps calm your body and mind, like hitting a reset button when you're feeling stressed.

Visualization techniques also offer a powerful way toward peace of mind. Picture yourself in a serene setting, such as a quiet forest or a sunlit beach. Close your eyes and imagine the details: the scent of pine needles or the sound of waves gently lapping the shore. This imaginative escape can be a soothing retreat from stressors.

Guided imagery is like a relaxing upgrade to regular visualization. You listen to calming stories or audio that help you unwind and let your mind take a break. You can find many of these online or in apps; it's an easy way to relax and recharge.

Progressive muscle relaxation is another technique that helps release physical tension stored in your body. This technique involves gradually tensing and relaxing different muscle groups. Begin at your toes and work your way up to your head at a steady pace. For each muscle group, inhale slowly and thoroughly as you tense the muscles for about five seconds, then exhale as you release the tension. This process helps ease physical tightness and stress, leaving you feeling calm and refreshed.

Picture yourself comfortable in a quiet space, free from distractions. As you go through each step, notice how your body feels lighter and more at ease. If you stick with it, the practice becomes almost meditative, helping to clear mental clutter while soothing physical discomforts.

Interactive Exercise: Creating Your Relaxation Routine

Take a moment to consider which relaxation techniques sound most effective to you. Is it deep breathing, visualization, or progressive muscle relaxation? Try each method daily for a few minutes over the next week, noting which is most effective. Incorporate your chosen method into a routine, using it whenever stress strikes or as part of winding down before bedtime.

These relaxation techniques offer more than temporary relief from stress. They provide tools to nurture long-term mental resilience and emotional well-being. By practicing regularly, you increase your self-awareness and build an inner calm that can more easily guide you through life's challenges.

Healthy Outlets for Emotional Expression

Imagine having a blank canvas in front of you, waiting for the first stroke of color. Engaging in creative activities like drawing or painting can be a powerful way to express emotions that words sometimes can't capture. The swirling of colors on a palette, the texture of the paintbrush against the canvas, is an expression of allowing feelings to flow freely.

When you're overwhelmed, picking up a pen or brush might be an excellent way to channel those emotions. Writing poetry or journaling can serve a similar purpose. Think of journaling as having a conversation with yourself, where you can share your thoughts without fear of judgment. The paper listens and absorbs everything, from confusion to clarity.

Physical activity is another incredible outlet for emotion regulation. Picture yourself hitting the pavement for a walk or run. As your feet pound the ground, stress and tension dissolve with each step. The endorphins released during exercise act like nature's mood lifters, transforming a bad day into one with possible silver linings.

Team sports offer social support and shared goals, while individual workouts allow for self-reflection and the opportunity to challenge yourself. Both can be beneficial depending on what you need at the moment. Yoga and tai chi offer more than just physical benefits; they provide a space for mindfulness, allowing you to center your thoughts and emotions.

Music and dance therapy are also great methods of emotional expression. Have you ever turned up your favorite song and danced around your room? It's liberating. Music can excite emotions and bring joy or comfort when needed. Creating playlists that reflect your emotional state can help you process feelings, offering a soundtrack to your life. Dance allows you to release pent-up energy and emotions through movement. It doesn't matter if you're in rhythm; it's about letting go and feeling the music move through you.

Sharing emotions with others is vital for emotional health. Think of it like opening a window to let fresh air into a stuffy room. Talking to friends or family members about what you're experiencing offers relief and perspective. Trusted individuals can provide support, helping you feel less isolated in your struggles.

Participating in support groups or peer circles creates a safe space for sharing, providing you with a place where you're heard and understood. These groups can offer insights from others who've faced similar challenges, providing comfort in shared experiences.

The beauty of these outlets is their flexibility and accessibility. Whether you prefer the solitude of writing or the energy of a group, there's an option that suits your needs. The key is finding what works for you and making it part of your routine. These activities help manage stress and enhance self-esteem by fostering creativity, connection, and self-awareness.

Creating is more than just an activity; it's a form of communication that bridges the gap between internal experience and external expression. When you engage in creative outlets, you're telling your story in a way that feels true to you. It's an opportunity to explore emotions freely and navigate life's complexities with imagination and courage.

Physical activity also builds resilience, teaching discipline and perseverance. Each time you push through fatigue or challenge yourself with new goals, you strengthen your body and mind. This resilience spills over into other areas of life, equipping you with tools to handle whatever comes your way.

Music and dance connect us to ourselves and others in unique ways. They offer joy, reflection, and healing, reminding us of our shared humanity. Through these art forms, we find common ground, understanding that emotions are universal, even if our stories differ.

Social support grounds us when life feels overwhelming. It reminds us we're not alone on this path; others walk alongside us, ready to lend an ear or shoulder when needed. This connection is what makes navigating life's challenges not just possible but meaningful.

Embracing these healthy outlets for emotional expression provides more than temporary relief; it fosters growth, self-discovery, and empowerment. Whether through creativity, physical activity, music, dance, or social connections, these activities enrich our lives with purpose and joy. They remind us that even during chaos or uncertainty, we have the power to create beauty and find peace within ourselves.

Crafting Your Coping Tools

Everyone handles stress differently. What works wonders for one person might not have the same effect for another. It is essential to identify what helps you manage stress. Reflect on moments when you felt overwhelmed. What activities or strategies brought you relief? Was it a quiet walk in nature or a good book that took you to another world? By understanding these past experiences, you can start piecing together the best tools for you.

Experimentation is key here. Don't be afraid to try new techniques or activities. Maybe a friend swears by meditation, but you've never tried. Or perhaps you've always been curious about how yoga could calm your mind. Dive into these experiences with an open mind. You might stumble upon something that feels just right to ease your stress. Remember, it's all about finding what fits comfortably within your life.

Equipping yourself with a coping toolkit can be incredibly beneficial. Think of it as a personalized first-aid kit for your mental well-being. Include items like a journal and pens, perfect for jotting down thoughts or drawing when words aren't enough. A stress ball or fidget spinner can provide relief, grounding you in the present moment. These items act as physical reminders of your ability to manage stress effectively.

Flexibility is crucial in coping strategies. Life is ever-changing, and what works today might not be as effective tomorrow. Update your toolkit regularly to reflect your current needs and experiences. You may have discovered a new breathing technique that helps calm your nerves; add that to your list! Being adaptable ensures you have practical tools on hand whenever you need them.

Regular evaluation of your coping strategies is essential to ensure their effectiveness. Keep a simple list where you note stress levels and the outcomes of different coping methods you've tried. This practice helps track what works best and highlights areas needing adjustment. Personal growth means evolving strategies, so stay open to feedback from yourself and those close to you who might offer valuable insights.

Exercise: Building Your Coping Toolkit

Take some time this week to create your coping toolkit. Gather physical items that will help you, such as art supplies, calming teas, or favorite books, and place them in a dedicated box or bag. Keep a list of which activities or tools help ease your stress and include them in your routine. Revisit and update this toolkit as needed.

As this chapter on healthy coping mechanisms draws to a close, remember that crafting personalized tools empowers you to help manage stress more effectively. Understanding what brings you relief and peace creates a foundation for resilience and self-discovery. The journey of managing stress is ongoing, but with each step taken, you strengthen your ability to face challenges head-on.

In the next chapter, we'll explore goal-setting and time-management skills, equipping you with techniques to organize your life efficiently and further reduce stress. With the right strategies, you'll be ready to tackle life's demands confidently with a clear mind.

Chapter 8

Goal Setting and Achievement

Setting S.M.A.R.T. Goals: A Blueprint for Success

Imagine you're going on a road trip without a map. It's thrilling at first, but as you get into unfamiliar territory, you soon find yourself lost, unsure of your destination. Setting goals without a clear framework is much like that aimless journey.

Never Underestimate The Power Of A Childhood Dream

S.M.A.R.T. goals offer a structured path to achievement. The acronym stands for Specific, Measurable, Achievable, Relevant, and Time-bound, a formula to ensure your goals are well-defined and attainable (Atlassian, n.d.). Being specific means zeroing in on precisely what you want to accomplish. Instead of saying, "I want to be healthier," specify it as "I want to run a 5K."

Measurable goals have clear criteria for tracking progress. For example, setting a target to run three times a week might be a good goal. Achievable goals are realistic, considering your current abilities and resources. They're about stretching yourself but not setting yourself up for failure. Relevant goals resonate with your values and priorities, ensuring they're worthwhile. Lastly, being Time-bound means setting a deadline to maintain focus and a sense of urgency.

Transforming vague hopes and ideas into S.M.A.R.T. goals can be a game-changer. Consider the difference between "I want to do better in school" and "I will improve my math grade by studying an extra hour each day for the next month." The second statement is precise, trackable, and more likely to lead to success. With this framework, you create a roadmap that guides you toward achievement, helping you focus on what truly matters.

To aid in setting your S.M.A.R.T. goals, I've included a S.M.A.R.T. handy worksheet at the end of Chapter 12 with prompts for each section. Start by identifying what you want to achieve and why it's essential. Then, break it down using the S.M.A.R.T. criteria (Atlassian, n.d.). This exercise helps clarify your objectives, turning them from abstract ideas into concrete plans. As you fill out the worksheet, you'll gain insight into the steps needed to reach your goals and how to measure your progress along the way.

Clear goal-setting offers numerous benefits beyond just planning. Research shows that well-defined goals enhance focus and motivation, leading to higher achievement rates (The Behavioral Wellness Group, n.d.). When you know what you're working toward, staying committed and driving toward it takes less effort.

There are many stories about individuals who've transformed their lives through the S.M.A.R.T. approach. One athlete I worked with wanted to improve their free-throw shooting percentage. By using this method, they gained confidence and eventually increased their consistency by setting specific goals for practice sessions and feedback.

Aligning your goals with personal values is crucial for making sure they hold meaning and significance to you. Your goals should reflect your interests and beliefs, making you more likely to stay motivated and engaged. Start by identifying your core values. What truly matters to you? It could be creativity, community, sports, or learning (Momentum Psychology, n.d.). Reflect on past goals and consider whether they aligned with these values. If not, think about how you can adjust future objectives to better match what's important to you.

Reflection Section: Aligning Goals with Values

Take some time to journal about your values and how they influence your goals. Use the following prompts:

1. What are three core values that guide your decisions?
2. How do these values align with your current goals?
3. Can you make any adjustments to reflect these values in your future planning?

Aligning goals with values enhances motivation and brings more profound satisfaction upon achievement. Each success becomes more meaningful when you pursue what resonates with your true self. Moreover, this alignment ensures that you're not just chasing external expectations but living authentically according to your principles.

By setting specific, measurable, achievable, relevant, and time-bound goals (S.M.A.R.T.), you're equipping yourself with the tools needed for success. These goals guide your efforts and focus, ensuring you're on track to achieve what truly matters to you.

Breaking Down Goals into Manageable Steps

When you think about a substantial goal, it can often feel like standing at the foot of a tall mountain, your eyes tracing its towering peaks and your heart fluttering with uncertainty about how to get to the top. This overwhelming sensation may cause you to stop before you even start. However, there is a strategy, almost like a hidden art, that involves breaking down that big goal into smaller, simpler steps.

Picture this like slicing a pizza; eating one piece at a time is far less challenging than attempting to devour the entire pie in one go. Dissecting your goal into more manageable pieces gradually transforms it from an impossible challenge into a series of manageable tasks. You can navigate this journey one piece at a time.

Imagine your ultimate goal is to write a novel. At first glance, composing an entire book can seem too difficult. Instead, if you focus on one chapter at a time, then narrow your focus down further to pages and eventually to paragraphs, the enormity of the task lessens considerably. This method simplifies the task into bite-sized portions and provides frequent encouragement and motivation as you reach each tiny milestone.

Practical strategies, such as creating a task ranking, can be incredibly beneficial in this rewarding journey. Begin with the primary tasks that directly influence your main objective. Secondary tasks, on the other hand, serve to support these primary tasks, offering a structured roadmap that navigates you from the starting point to the finish line.

Mind maps can help you visually organize your goal's smaller parts and determine how they interconnect. By laying out these steps visually, you can see the pathway more clearly and identify the intersections where your efforts on each step should meet.

With various tasks in front of you, it's important to figure out which demands immediate attention. By prioritizing tasks based on their urgency and overall impact, you ensure that your focus is on what is genuinely significant at present.

Imagine a simple chart that helps you sort your to-dos by their urgency and importance. It shows you what needs your attention right now and what can wait, so you can stay focused and use your time where it really matters.

Having a solid game plan makes it way easier to reach your goals. Just like in sports, when you break things down into steps and set clear targets, you stay focused and in control. Writing out what you need to do, setting deadlines, and checking your progress can help you stay motivated and hold yourself accountable. It's like running drills you practice, track how you're doing, and make changes when something's not working.

Calendar-based planning can be remarkably effective for those who prefer a more traditional approach. By scheduling tasks on a calendar or in a planner, you ensure that your time is allocated effectively, avoiding last-minute scrambles and significantly enhancing your time management skills.

Think of your big goal like the final level of a video game. At first, it might seem impossible, but when you break it into smaller missions, it gets way easier (and more fun). Every task you complete is like leveling up, giving you more confidence and momentum. The trick is turning those huge, overwhelming goals into bite-sized challenges. That way, you're not just beating the game, you're actually enjoying every step of the quest.

Celebrating Small Wins: Motivation Boosters

Picture finally making it to the top of a rugged hill after a long, challenging climb. You stop, catch your breath, and look around. It might not be the highest mountain in the world, but the view is still awesome and totally worth it.

Celebrating small wins on your journey through life is like enjoying that view. It involves acknowledging and appreciating the effort and determination it took to get there, however minor it might seem in the grand scheme of your hopes and dreams. This kind of recognition is a powerful tool for positive motivation. It's like giving yourself a much-deserved pat on the back. This can make all the difference in preserving and enhancing your momentum.

When you recognize your progress, your brain actually rewards you by releasing dopamine, the chemical that makes you feel good and keeps you motivated to keep going. This can be seen in the real-world experiences of many successful individuals who attribute their achievements to the consistent celebration of each milestone, no matter how small it may appear.

I once had an athlete who came up with a fun way to stay motivated. She treated herself to her favorite ice cream every time she finished a chapter in her textbook. It might seem like a small thing, but it kept her going and gave her something to look forward to. By the time exams came around, she crushed it.

Celebrating your wins is all about creativity and making it personal. It doesn't have to be some big, over-the-top moment; what matters most is choosing something that feels meaningful to you. Maybe it's grabbing your favorite snack, picking up a new book, or just taking a break to do something you love without distractions. These little rewards can keep you motivated and remind you that every step forward deserves to be noticed. Whether it's in sports, school, or life.

Journaling is another great tool for celebration. It allows you to document your achievements while reflecting on how they have boosted your self-confidence, step by step. This practice can be deeply fulfilling, providing a reflective view to help you appreciate how each victory nudges you closer to your larger goals. These reflections, when recorded in your journal, can serve as motivational reminders to get you through more difficult times along your journey.

Reflection is a big part of celebration. By devoting time to reflecting on your accomplishments, you deepen your sense of achievement and learn from your successes. Dive into reflective journaling prompts with questions such as, "What did this win teach me?" or "How has this progress changed my perspective?"

Asking these types of questions can lead to important insights. Group discussions with friends provide an additional platform for mutual celebration. Engaging in conversations about victories boosts joy while strengthening bonds through shared experiences and support.

Celebrating regularly can shift your mindset and keep you motivated. By setting weekly or monthly goals that include reflection and celebration, you ensure a steady and consistent acknowledgment of your progress. Use visual aids like progress charts, mapping your growth, to celebrate your milestones. Observing your progress can be strongly motivating, as a constant reminder of the distance you've traveled.

Ultimately, celebrating these seemingly small victories becomes more than just morale-boosting. It's a crucial activity that builds resilience and reinforces productive habits. It becomes a reminder that success is truly an accumulation of little steps rather than occasional giant leaps. Over time, these small celebrations become part of your daily life, creating an environment of growth, positivity, and uplifting energy.

Overcoming Procrastination and Staying Focused

Procrastination often sneaks in when you least expect it. One minute, you're determined to tackle your task; the next, you're scrolling through your phone or rearranging your room for the umpteenth time. It drains your time and productivity, but understanding where it comes from can help you conquer it.

Sometimes it's the fear of failing that holds you back, like a voice in your head saying it's better to avoid it than to risk not getting it right. Perfectionism makes you set impossibly high standards that make starting seem overwhelming. These triggers create a cycle of delay that leads to stress and missed opportunities.

Consider how procrastination comes up in daily life. It could be the assignment due tomorrow that you've barely started or the upcoming exam you've yet to study for. The consequences ripple through your schedule, creating last-minute cramming and rushed results. However, recognizing these patterns is the first step toward change.

To work through procrastination, equip yourself with practical strategies. Time management techniques like the Pomodoro Technique can be game-changers. This method involves working in focused bursts, typically 25 minutes long, followed by short breaks to refresh your mind. It's a way to trick your brain into productivity by promising a reward, in this case, a break, after a brief work period. Setting deadlines, even for tasks without set ones, creates a sense of urgency that can propel you into action.

Accountability buddies also offer support by adding a layer of responsibility. Sharing your goals with someone else means you're more likely to stay on track because someone else is counting on you. This shared journey transforms an isolating battle into a collaborative effort.

Developing habits that enhance focus can further build your defenses against distraction. Start by creating a study environment free from distractions like your phone or cluttered spaces. A tidy space promotes a tidy mind, allowing you to concentrate fully on the task.

Mindfulness practices, such as meditation or deep breathing exercises, can sharpen your focus by training your mind to remain present. They teach you to recognize when your attention drifts and gently guide it back.

Self-discipline is what holds it all together. A lot of successful people don't just rely on talent; they credit their success to staying consistent and putting in the work. Think about athletes who wake up before sunrise to train for hours. This story shows that discipline is what turns goals into real results.

Daily challenges can increase self-discipline by clearly defining expectations and reinforcing habits. A commitment contract is a promise you make to yourself or others, outlining specific actions you'll take and the consequences if you don't follow through. Daily challenges encourage consistency by setting achievable tasks that build momentum over time.

As you wrap up this chapter, remember that overcoming procrastination and improving focus are ongoing processes that require patience and practice. By understanding procrastination's roots and working on strategies to counteract it, you're laying the foundation for continuous success.

In the next chapter, we'll explore how managing emotions can further enhance your ability to achieve goals and improve relationships. This emotional intelligence is key to navigating life's complexities gracefully and with empathy.

Chapter 9

Preparation, Planning and Time Management

The Importance of Time Management

Patrick is an excellent student in many ways. He's smart and often knows the answers to questions raised in class. However, he struggles with getting his homework done on time. He always has the idea that he'll have time to finish it, but he can't quite juggle all the things on his schedule, including friends, family time, and football practice.

By the time Patrick finally gets around to his homework, it's often the night before it's due, and he has to rush. Sometimes he doesn't get the assignment done at all, and when he does, it's often not his best work. Because of this, his grades suffer.

Imagine yourself standing on the sidewalk overlooking a big, busy city. Each building you see symbolizes a task or duty, ranging from school assignments and practice to family time. Finding your way efficiently through to the other side would be overwhelming without a detailed map.

Picture time management as that essential map, providing guidance and direction through your daily life with intention and clarity. Time management is more than just sticking to a schedule; it involves maximizing your available time to stay organized and feel less overwhelmed.

Effective time management can totally change your daily routine. Picture a highly organized study schedule that supports you in managing assignments, allowing more downtime for enjoyment and relaxation. A structured plan lowers the probability of procrastination, significantly reducing anxiety over upcoming deadlines.

As a result, this paves the way for better productivity and performance. Mastering time management allows you to complete tasks more effectively, unlocking precious time for your goals and interests.

Ignoring time management can trigger a ripple effect of stress and anxiety. Visualize a pile of unfinished assignments growing day after day, with each one further raising your stress levels. Without properly managing your time, deadlines approach, causing panic as you hurry to finish tasks right before they're due. Along with worse grades at school, your performance in extracurricular activities and even your social interactions could suffer under relentless pressure.

The silver lining is that mastering time management can significantly transform your mental health. By skillfully organizing your day, you can reduce feelings of being swamped. A thoughtful plan can give you a reassuring sense of control over your life, enhancing both confidence and overall well-being.

Picture opening your eyes each day with a clear vision of your tasks and a strategic approach to completing them; this type of structure has a calming effect, elevating your mood and mental resilience.

Consider Sam, a dedicated student-athlete excelling in both sports and academics. By efficiently crafting a study timetable balanced with his practice sessions, Sam makes enough time for both schoolwork and athletic training without compromising sleep or time with friends and family. This balanced schedule empowers him to keep up excellent grades while reaching new heights in sports. It also keeps his stress levels in check.

Reflection Section: Your Time Management Journey

Pause momentarily to reflect on your time management skills. Recall a recent instance when you felt overwhelmed by tasks or deadlines. Write down the things that contributed to these feelings and try to think of one concrete change you could make to refine your time management approach.

Effective time management isn't just about arranging your schedule; it's about opening the door to creativity, relaxation, and personal growth. It strikes a balance where productivity aligns seamlessly with peace of mind, empowering you to navigate life's challenges more confidently. Embrace the strategies that authentically resonate with you and observe as they improve your calendar's efficiency and your overall happiness and sense of accomplishment.

As you explore deeper into the advantages of time management, remember that the goal is not perfection but continual progress. Every small step toward improved time management can make a big difference. So, start drawing your own map and start this journey with optimism.

Setting Priorities

Picture this: you wake up to a day filled with school projects, practice, a family dinner, and a group chat buzzing with friends planning a weekend hangout. Everything is screaming for your attention at once. That's where prioritization steps in, essentially acting as your superhero cape. Prioritizing isn't about doing everything; it's about doing the right things at the right time.

Imagine sorting tasks into two boxes: one for urgent and another for necessary. Urgent tasks demand immediate action, like finishing tonight's homework or responding to a friend in need. On the other hand, necessary tasks might not scream for attention but hold significant long-term value, like preparing for that big exam next week or working on your college application. Balancing these is key to managing your day and guiding you toward your bigger life goals.

Figuring out what to tackle first can feel overwhelming. Meet the Eisenhower Box, a nifty tool for categorizing tasks by urgency and importance. It divides your tasks into four quadrants: do first, schedule, delegate, and don't do. This helps you identify what requires immediate attention and what could be scheduled for later or passed on to someone else. It's like having a personal assistant who knows what's best for you.

Pair this tool with goal-setting exercises that align tasks with your objectives and have a recipe for productivity. When you see what aligns with your goals, prioritizing becomes second nature.

Handling multiple responsibilities can feel like juggling flaming torches while riding a unicycle. But with strategies like time blocking, you can manage competing priorities without dropping the ball. Dedicate specific chunks of time to focus all your attention on one task or project. This method increases concentration and prevents the chaos of multitasking.

Another strategy is delegation; don't hesitate to share responsibilities when possible. Teamwork can lighten your load significantly, whether teaming up with a classmate for a group project or asking family members for help with chores.

Flexibility plays a huge role in effective prioritization. Life is unpredictable; priorities change, and that's perfectly okay. Regularly reassess what's on your plate to make sure it aligns with your current goals and circumstances. Weekly reviews are a great habit to develop; they allow you to adjust priorities based on progress and new developments. Reflective journaling can be an excellent companion in this process.

Imagine rolling out of bed each morning knowing what needs your attention that day. You feel in control and ready to tackle whatever comes your way. That's the power of setting priorities, creating a sense of order during the emotional whirlwinds, and ensuring you're not just busy but productive in ways that truly matter.

To keep this momentum going, consider engaging in a weekly reflection session where you write down what's working, what's not, and how you can improve. You may have discovered that dedicating an hour every morning to studying boosts your grades or that scheduling your free time improves your mood and energy levels. Use these insights to tweak your priorities as needed.

It's important to remember that prioritization adapts as your life evolves and as new challenges emerge. It empowers you to make informed decisions about where to invest your time and energy, ensuring you're always moving toward what matters most.

Ultimately, setting priorities isn't just about checking off tasks on a list; it's about crafting a life that aligns with your values and goals. It's about making choices that bring you closer to where you want to be while enjoying the journey.

Tools for Effective Time Management

Let's talk about some tools that can help you get a grip on your time. Picture having a trusty sidekick, ready to help you tackle your tasks and keep your schedule running smoothly. Digital apps are fantastic for task management. Think of them as your digital bulletin boards, where you can pin tasks, set deadlines, and track progress. These apps allow you to create lists, assign tasks, and collaborate. It's like having a digital command center in your pocket, with notifications and updates to keep you on track.

For those who prefer to work on paper, planner notebooks and journals offer a satisfying way to organize your thoughts and your schedule. There's something about writing things down that helps them stick in your mind. Bullet journals can offer a creative outlet as well. You can use different colors and layouts to categorize tasks and visualize your schedule. They're great for those who like a bit of personalization and creativity in their planning process.

Calendar apps are another powerful tool you can try. They provide an overview of your week or month at a glance, making it easy to spot potential scheduling conflicts. Features like reminders and alerts ensure you never miss a necessary appointment or deadline. These apps sync across all your devices to access your schedule anytime, anywhere, so you're always up to date with your plans.

Setting up recurring tasks and reminders in your apps is a game-changer. Whether it's a weekly study session or a monthly meeting, having these reminders pop up helps keep you on top of things without manually tracking everything.

However, with the benefits of technology come potential downsides; digital distractions are everywhere. Using apps with built-in focus features can help minimize interruptions. These features often block social media notifications or limit access to distracting sites during study sessions. Setting specific times for checking emails and notifications is another strategy to help maintain focus. This way, you aren't constantly pulled away by the ding of a new message while trying to concentrate on something important.

With these tools, managing your time becomes less of a chore and more of an organized system that supports you in reaching your goals. Whatever tools you choose can offer unique benefits. It's all about finding what works best for you in your routine.

The trick is consistency, using these tools regularly until they become second nature. Over time, this habit will help smooth out the bumps in your schedule and make even the busiest days feel more manageable. Remember that the goal isn't to fill every moment with tasks but to create space for what truly matters to you.

With practice and persistence, these tools can help transform how you manage your time, allowing you to focus more on what brings joy and fulfillment into your life. Whether digital or not, there's a tool out there ready to help streamline your days and maximize productivity without sacrificing peace of mind.

Balancing School, Activities, and Social Life

Imagine standing at a crossroads, with several paths leading to significant aspects of your life: schoolwork, extracurricular activities, and spending time with friends. Each path calls for your attention, and choosing which one to follow at any given moment isn't always straightforward.

For teens, balancing these areas of life can feel like juggling while walking on a tightrope. It's a balancing act where time conflicts surface, pitting school assignments against after-school activities.

Picture this: you have a crucial athletic game scheduled when you're supposed to be finishing a science project. Social pressures add another layer when friends make last-minute plans for outings that clash with your planned study sessions, pulling your attention in multiple competing directions.

Finding balance starts with creating a structured weekly schedule. This is not just any checklist; it's your week's visual roadmap. It involves assigning specific time slots for each essential component of your life, much like fitting together pieces of a puzzle. This ensures that time is allocated effectively, so you don't feel overwhelmed.

When creating your schedule, remember to set reasonable boundaries. It's important to protect quality time for personal interests by asserting the power to say no when necessary. It's perfectly okay to opt out of a social hangout if you must fully focus on preparing for a big test or practice, or require some precious time to relax.

Self-care is a key component of maintaining balance. After all, you can't pour from an empty cup, right? Incorporating regular breaks is an absolute necessity. Make sure to leave time for rest in your daily routine.

Whether you prefer a stroll through the park, reading a book, or practicing yoga, these activities hold the magical potential to recharge your mental and physical batteries. They revitalize your energy and enhance productivity when you return to your tasks feeling renewed. Stress-reduction activities work wonders for your mental health, acting as a powerful release valve for built-up tension and anxiety.

Sophia is a high school senior with a seemingly endless list of responsibilities and activities. She managed to keep her grades up while participating in the drama club and volunteering her time and love at the local animal shelter. How did Ava do it? Through the creation of a weekly schedule that balanced her commitments with clarity. She devoted specific time slots to homework, rehearsals, and volunteering.

On weekends, she set time aside for friends and family gatherings. Sophia's true secret was her sharp awareness of her limits and knowing when to step back to recharge herself. By setting practical boundaries and emphasizing self-care, she successfully maintained a balance between her responsibilities and personal life.

Reflection Section: Your Balance Check

Take a moment to think about the current balance across your life's different responsibilities and activities. Are there particular areas that feel overwhelming or neglected? Write down one change you can make next week to create more balance.

Balancing different areas of life isn't about chasing a state of perfection but finding a unique rhythm that works best for your needs and circumstances. Don't worry if some weeks are more intensely school-focused while others allow you to relax and socialize more. The key is adaptability, adjusting your plans and expectations as needed, all while keeping your biggest priorities firmly in check.

Ultimately, balancing school, activities, and social life is about more than fitting everything into your calendar. It's about designing a life that gives you a sense of fulfillment and productivity without making sacrifices to your well-being. As you fine-tune these balancing skills, you'll notice that the chaos of competing demands gradually transforms into a routine that supports your personal growth and joy.

In the next chapter, we will explore emotional intelligence, a vital component in managing relationships with others and deepening our understanding of ourselves. By consciously enhancing these skills, you'll improve how you interact with others and gain insight into navigating your own complex emotions.

Chapter 10

Enhancing Social Skills

The Art of Conversation: Engaging Effectively

Imagine walking into a room full of people, your heart thumping like a drum. Conversations buzz around you like a hive of bees, and you wonder how to jump in without awkwardness. The art of conversation isn't just about talking; it's about engaging with others in a way that makes everyone feel valued.

Active engagement means listening and showing genuine interest in the people you talk to. When someone knows you're genuinely interested, it opens the door to a meaningful connection. It is not about pretending; it's about being present and engaged.

Start by asking open-ended questions, ones that can't be answered with a simple "yes" or "no." Instead of asking, "Did you enjoy the movie?" try, "What did you think of the movie's ending?" This allows others to share their thoughts and feelings more fully. It's like offering them a canvas and a set of paints, allowing them to express their ideas. This approach shows that you're interested in their perspective.

Maintaining a balanced dialogue is crucial. Picture a seesaw; the balance is lost if one side is too heavy. Similarly, conversations require a balance between speaking and listening. Please share your thoughts, but also give others space to express theirs. This mutual exchange keeps the conversation lively and engaging, creating an environment where everyone feels heard.

Active listening is key to enhancing conversation. It involves more than just hearing words; it's about understanding the speaker's message and emotions. Practice reflective listening by summarizing what you've heard. For example, if someone is excited about a new hobby, you might respond, "It sounds like painting brings you a lot of joy," showing that you're paying attention and value what they're saying.

Practicing active listening can lead to powerful personal growth. A straightforward exercise involves pairing up with a friend and sharing a story, while the other friend summarizes the key points. This activity sharpens your ability to listen deeply and respond thoughtfully, strengthening your conversational skills.

Conversational anxiety is common, especially in unfamiliar settings. Anxiety can make your mind race or leave you tongue-tied. To combat this, prepare topics of interest before social events. Consider recent news stories, books you've read, or interests you share with those attending. Having these topics on hand provides a safety net, boosting your confidence to engage.

Practicing conversation starters and icebreakers can ease nerves. Simple phrases like "How was your weekend?" or "Have you tried any new hobbies lately?" can open the door to deeper conversations. These starters are like keys unlocking conversational doors, inviting others to step in and share.

Confidence builds through regular practice. Consider joining clubs or groups focused on public speaking or debate. These environments provide supportive spaces to hone your skills and gain confidence in expressing yourself. You'll strengthen your communication abilities and meet others who share your interests.

Role-playing with friends is another effective way to simulate real-life conversations. Create scenarios where you practice initiating and maintaining dialogue, offering a safe space to experiment with different approaches and techniques. The more you practice, the more natural these interactions become.

Interactive Element: Conversation Role-Playing Exercise

Pair up with a friend or family member and choose a scenario, perhaps meeting someone new at a party or discussing a shared interest. Take turns playing different roles, focusing on asking open-ended questions, and practicing active listening. Reflect on what worked well and areas for improvement.

Remember, you can learn and refine the art of conversation over time. Each interaction offers an opportunity to practice, grow, and connect with others on a deeper level. As you continue to sharpen these skills, you'll find yourself navigating social situations quickly and confidently, building meaningful relationships that improve your life in countless ways.

Reading Social Cues and Body Language

Imagine standing quietly in a corner at a party, unsure whether to approach a group chatting nearby. You notice their gestures, their laughter, and the way they lean in as they speak. While verbal communication uses words to convey messages, non-verbal cues often reveal what's left unsaid. A smile might express warmth, while crossed arms can indicate discomfort. These signals can tell a story all on their own, complementing or even contradicting spoken words.

To navigate social interactions effectively, you need to interpret social cues accurately. Start by observing facial expressions. For example, when someone's eyes light up with excitement or narrow with doubt, those small changes can reveal what they're truly feeling beneath the surface."

Practice by watching movies or going people-watching in a park, focusing on how expressions change with emotions. Observe gestures and posture, too. Open gestures like spreading arms are inviting, while closed ones suggest withdrawal. Being aware of this helps you respond appropriately, offering comfort when you sense unease or sharing in someone's joy when they're happy.

Doing some exercises to learn this skill can be both fun and helpful. Consider an activity where you and a friend take turns expressing emotions without speaking, and figure out each other's feelings based solely on body language. This practice sharpens your ability to read non-verbal cues and enhances your empathic understanding. Understanding these low-key signals can make interactions smoother, allowing for more connected and meaningful relationships.

However, it's important to remember that body language isn't universal; it varies across cultures. Direct eye contact is a sign of confidence in some places, while it is disrespectful in others. Personal space can also differ; what feels comfortable for one culture might feel intrusive to another. Being aware of these cultural differences helps prevent misunderstandings and encourages respectful interactions. When in doubt, observe and adapt to the comfort levels of those around you.

While reading social cues is vital, being mindful of your body language is equally important. The way you present yourself can influence how others see you. Take a moment to think about your typical gestures and posture. Do you often cross your arms when nervous? Are you aware of maintaining eye contact? By reflecting on these habits, you gain insight into how you might come across to others.

Practice maintaining an upright posture with relaxed shoulders to project confidence and openness. Use hand gestures to emphasize points when speaking, but avoid overdoing it to maintain balance. A genuine smile can work wonders in conveying warmth and approachability. Experiment with these techniques in front of a mirror or during everyday interactions to see what feels natural yet effective.

Self-Assessment Activity: Personal Body Language Habits

Take a few minutes each day to observe your body language in different settings: at school, on teams, with friends, and at home. Note any patterns or habits that stand out and consider how they might influence your interactions. Reflect on adjustments that could enhance your non-verbal communication.

Improving your non-verbal communication skills enhances your interaction with others and boosts your confidence in social situations. As you become more in tune with the silent language of gestures and expressions, you'll connect with people on a deeper level, building relationships that thrive on mutual understanding and respect.

Building a Supportive Friend Network

Having a strong network of friends feels like having a safety net that catches you when life tries to knock you down. Supportive friendships enhance emotional well-being and build resilience, offering a sense of belonging that can help you navigate the ups and downs of life. Imagine having friends who celebrate your achievements and stand by you during challenging times. This support is invaluable, helping you deal with stress and boosting happiness.

One key benefit of having a diverse and supportive social circle is the variety of perspectives it brings. When your friends come from different backgrounds, they introduce you to new ideas and ways of thinking, broadening your horizons and helping you grow. It's like having a passport to other worlds, each friend offering insights into their unique experiences. This diversity enriches your life and enables you to develop a more well-rounded view of the world.

Building meaningful connections starts with finding common ground. Shared interests and values lay the foundation for lasting friendships. Whether bonding over a love for music, sports, or books, these similarities create a sense of connection that makes interactions enjoyable. Consider joining clubs or groups that align with your passions. This helps you meet like-minded individuals and provides opportunities to engage in activities you love.

Starting and maintaining friendships takes effort and intention. Start by contacting people who share your interests and inviting them to participate in activities or events. Be genuine in your approach, showing interest in their lives and listening actively. As friendships develop, grow them by staying in touch and making time for regular interactions, sending a quick text, or planning an event together.

Trust and communication are the cornerstones of any strong friendship. They are built and strengthened through consistent actions that demonstrate reliability and honesty. Be there for your friends when they need support, and show appreciation for their presence in your life. Open communication is equally important, allowing you to address misunderstandings before they spin out of control. When conflicts arise, approach them with empathy and a willingness to understand the other person's perspective.

To maintain trust, practice active listening and validate your friends' feelings. Acknowledge their emotions and offer reassurance that you're there for them, creating an environment where they feel safe sharing their thoughts without fear of judgment. When misunderstandings occur, address them openly and constructively. Use "I" statements to express how specific actions made you feel rather than placing blame.

Expanding your social network can also be achieved through community or extracurricular activities. Joining clubs, teams, or volunteer groups opens doors to new friendships while providing opportunities to contribute positively to your community. Being part of a team builds teamwork and collaboration, allowing you to work toward common goals with others who share your interests.

Participating in community events or workshops introduces you to a broader circle of potential friends. Attend local fairs, art exhibitions, or charity events to meet people who care about similar causes. These shared experiences create bonds that extend beyond surface-level interactions, allowing you to connect on a deeper level.

These activities expand your social circle and allow you to gain valuable teamwork, leadership, and communication skills. These skills enhance your personal growth and prepare you for the future, both personally and professionally.

Building a supportive friend network requires effort and intention, but the rewards are huge. The connections you form provide emotional support, companionship, and inspiration, essential ingredients for a fulfilling life. As you grow these relationships, remember that it's not about the number of friends you have but the quality of those connections that truly matter.

Involve yourself in activities that align with your passions and values, continuously seeking opportunities to meet new people and make meaningful friendships. With time and dedication, you'll surround yourself with friends who uplift and inspire you.

Navigating Group Dynamics with Ease

Understanding group dynamics is like learning to sail a ship; each person plays a role, steering the group toward success. Some are natural leaders, guiding the ship and ensuring everyone stays on course. Others might be mediators, smoothing over conflicts and keeping the peace. Then there are participants, the vital crew members who contribute ideas and energy to propel the group forward.

Effective group participation requires specific skills that help positively impact outcomes. Active group engagement is crucial; it means being physically and mentally present. It's about sharing ideas and knowing when to step back and let others take the floor. Collaboration is the key, where everyone's efforts blend into a harmony. You become an indispensable part of the team by focusing on the group's goals and how your strengths can support them.

Managing group conflict is an art form. When disagreements arise, it's essential to address them constructively. Acknowledge differing opinions and work toward a consensus that respects all viewpoints. A practical approach involves setting aside personal biases and focusing on solutions that benefit the group. Strategies like holding open discussions or using structured decision-making processes help resolve disagreements and keep the group moving forward.

Adaptability in group settings is key. Dynamic environments often require quick thinking and flexibility. Picture a successful group project where plans suddenly change. An environment where adaptability shines is about adjusting your sails when the wind shifts, ensuring you stay on course despite challenges. Being open-minded allows you to embrace new ideas and perspectives, enhancing the group's creativity.

Effective group dynamics also offer an opportunity for developing leadership skills. Leadership within a group context doesn't always mean being in charge; it's about inspiring others and making decisions that guide the group toward its goals. Leadership exercises can improve decision-making and delegation skills. Practice scenarios where you must choose the best action or assign tasks based on team members' strengths. These exercises build confidence and prepare you for real-life leadership opportunities.

Taking on leadership roles or being a captain within teams, school, or community groups provides practical experience. Volunteering to lead a project or organize an event allows you to put theory into practice, navigating real challenges while motivating and guiding your peers. These experiences strengthen your leadership abilities and boost your self-esteem, showing you can make a meaningful impact.

Interactive Element: Group Role Exploration Exercise

Gather a small group of friends or classmates and assign different roles, such as leader, mediator, or participant, for a mock project or discussion. Take turns rotating roles to experience different dynamics and understand each role's responsibilities.

As you navigate group dynamics, remember that each interaction offers growth and learning opportunities. Whether leading a project or supporting a team member, these experiences enrich your skillset and prepare you for future challenges. Embrace every role enthusiastically and open-mindedly, knowing your contributions make a difference.

This chapter has explored how understanding group dynamics can enhance social skills, preparing you for collaborative environments where teamwork thrives. As we transition into the next chapter on emotional intelligence, consider how these skills will complement your ability to connect with others on an emotional level, encouraging more meaningful relationships in all areas of life.

Chapter 11

Navigating the Digital World

Social Media and Self-Esteem

Imagine scrolling through your feed and seeing one perfect picture after another. People seem to be living their best lives, but is that reality? With its endless curated images and stories, Social media can help or hurt your self-esteem, depending on what you're seeing and how you see yourself.

On one hand, it offers a platform to connect with friends and like-minded individuals, making you feel less alone. On the other hand, it can create a pressure cooker of comparison, where likes and comments become a measure of self-worth. When your photo gets fewer likes than expected, it's easy to spiral into self-doubt, questioning your value or appeal (Child Mind Institute, n.d.).

The impact of social media goes beyond just counting likes. It often leads to comparing oneself with others, especially those portraying idealized lifestyles. This constant comparison can twist your perception of what's expected or attainable. The glossy images of vacations, perfect relationships, and flawless appearances can set unrealistic standards. Over time, this might lead to feelings of inadequacy or dissatisfaction with your life. But remember, these snapshots rarely show the whole picture behind the scenes.

Your online persona can also significantly shape your identity. Many teens feel like they must present a flawless image online, which can differ from their true selves. This disconnect creates an internal conflict between who you are and who you feel pressured to be. Maintaining multiple online identities can be exhausting and lead to anxiety over being "found out." The constant pressure to choose carefully a perfect image might keep you from appreciating your authentic self.

Unfortunately, social media isn't always a safe space. Cyberbullying is a harsh reality that can severely damage self-esteem. Hurtful comments or messages can linger in your thoughts, impacting how you see yourself. Recognizing signs of cyberbullying is crucial, whether it's repeated negative comments or exclusion from online groups.

Developing strategies to deal with online harassment is equally essential. These might include blocking bullies, reporting harmful behavior, or confiding in trusted friends or adults for support (The Jed Foundation, n.d.).

Despite these challenges, social media also holds the potential for positive influence. Used thoughtfully, it can be a tool for building self-esteem. Connecting with supportive communities offers a sense of belonging. These communities can be spaces for finding encouragement and shared experiences. Following inspirational accounts or content that aligns with your interests can uplift your mood and motivate personal growth.

To create a healthier relationship with social media, focus on connecting with positive influences. Choose carefully your feed to include content that educates or inspires you. Engage with posts that encourage growth and reflect values you aspire to live by. Doing so transforms social media from a source of stress into a platform for learning and self-improvement.

Reflection Section: Curate Your Feed

Take a moment to reflect on the accounts you follow and the content you engage with regularly. Are there accounts that make you feel inspired and happy? Or do some posts leave you feeling anxious or inadequate? Consider unfollowing sources that negatively impact your self-esteem and seek out those that provide positivity or education.

This digital space is yours to shape. By being mindful of your interactions and the content you consume, you can navigate social media in a way that enhances rather than diminishes your self-worth. Remember, the world you build online should reflect the support, understanding, and values you hold dear in real life.

Setting Boundaries Online

In this digital age, setting boundaries online is like drawing a line in the sand, marking what's yours to protect. It's crucial for maintaining mental health and well-being. The internet is endless, and without boundaries, it's easy to feel overwhelmed by the huge volume of information and interactions.

In this environment, protecting your privacy and personal information becomes extremely important. Oversharing online can attract the wrong kind of attention—or even put your information at risk. It's all about being smart with what you post and who sees it, so your personal life stays safe and private.

Overexposure to harmful content can also weigh heavily on your mind, leading to stress and anxiety. By setting clear limits on what you consume online, you create a healthier digital environment for yourself.

To establish healthy online habits, consider using app usage trackers to limit screen time. These tools can help you see where you're spending your time so you can adjust as needed. Scheduling regular digital breaks throughout your day is another effective strategy. Step away from screens to engage in offline activities like reading, exercising, or spending time with family and friends. These breaks refresh your mind and remind you of life beyond the screen.

Balance is key; by managing your online time wisely, you can enjoy the benefits of digital connectivity without feeling trapped by it.

Parental guidance plays a significant role in setting these digital boundaries. Open communication with parents about online activities encourages trust and understanding. Creating family agreements on screen time limits ensures everyone is on the same page.

Discussing safe online behavior and privacy settings can help protect against potential risks. By working together, families can create a supportive environment where teens feel secure in their online interactions. Parents offer valuable perspectives and can help navigate challenges you might encounter in the digital world.

Communicating your boundaries is just as important as setting them. When you're clear about your limits, you're less likely to feel pressured into situations that make you uncomfortable. Decreasing unnecessary group chats or setting clear limits on information sharing shows respect for yourself and your time.

For example, if a friend sends too many messages during study time, let them know you're focusing on schoolwork and will reply later. It's not about shutting people out but ensuring respect for your needs. Establishing these boundaries helps others understand your priorities and creates mutual respect that strengthens relationships.

Digital detoxes can complement these efforts by offering a reset when needed. In doing so, you might discover new interests or deepen your enjoyment of existing hobbies. This practice encourages reflection on your relationship with technology and its role. A well-timed detox can provide clarity and reinforce the importance of the boundaries you've set.

Being assertive in boundary setting isn't just about saying no; it's about confidently stating your needs and standing by them. It requires practice and sometimes courage, but the payoff is worth it. When you communicate openly and honestly about what you're comfortable with, you empower yourself and encourage others to do the same. This exchange creates a culture of respect and understanding that enhances all your interactions.

Setting boundaries online is an ongoing process that requires attention and intention. By protecting your privacy, limiting exposure to negativity, and maintaining a balanced digital life, you create a healthier online experience. Engaging openly with family and asserting yourself when necessary ensures these boundaries are respected and preserved. Remember, it's your digital space; make it work for you.

Digital Detox and Its Benefits

Carrie loves designing clothes and has a dream of one day owning her own fashion line. She posts photos of her creations on social media, but used to get so distracted with scrolling and bogged down with notifications that her focus suffered. After setting herself some much-needed limits and taking digital recharge when she needs them, Carrie is running a thriving business page, and her designs get a lot of positive engagement.

Imagine opening your eyes to a new day and, instead of reaching for your phone, you step outside to embrace the fresh air. That's what a digital recharge is all about: choosing to disconnect from screens intentionally. It's like giving your mind a much-needed vacation from the endless scroll. Technology plays a significant role in our lives, often shaping our mental health in ways we don't even notice. Taking breaks from screens allows you to reconnect with offline experiences and activities that bring joy and fulfillment. Whether reading your favorite book, playing an instrument, or simply enjoying a walk in nature, these moments remind you of life's simpler pleasures.

But how do you know when it's time to take a break? You might notice signs like digital fatigue or burnout. It might be time for a detox if you find yourself constantly tired, no matter how much you sleep, or feeling overwhelmed by the endless notifications on your phone. Perhaps you're experiencing headaches or eye strain from hours spent staring at screens. These physical symptoms often accompany mental exhaustion caused by information overload. Recognizing these signs is the first step toward reclaiming your well-being.

So, what's the best way to have a successful digital reset? Start by setting specific goals for screen-free time. Decide on a day or even a few hours when you commit to putting away your devices. During this time, engage in alternative activities that don't involve screens. Pick up a book you've meant to read or head outside for some fresh air and exercise.

Outdoor sports like cycling or hiking can be particularly refreshing, offering a change of scenery and a chance to connect with nature. You could also try cooking a new recipe or indulging in an art project.

The benefits of stepping away from screens go beyond just reducing stress. You'll likely notice improved focus and concentration as your brain breaks from constant multitasking. Without an endless stream of notifications pulling your attention in different directions, you can fully focus on your tasks and enjoy a deeper sense of accomplishment. Additionally, engaging in offline activities that bring joy and relaxation naturally boost happy brain signals, leaving you feeling more content and balanced.

A digital unplug doesn't require completely cutting yourself off from technology forever. It's about finding the right balance that allows you to enjoy the benefits of both digital and real-life experiences. Taking intentional breaks from screens will enable you to recharge mentally and emotionally. This practice improves your mental health and enhances your overall quality of life. You can then approach technology with renewed energy and focus.

Incorporating these breaks into your routine might feel challenging at first, but with a little effort, they can become a natural part of your life. Consider starting small, perhaps with an hour a day, then gradually extending the duration as you become more comfortable with the concept. You may even look forward to these digital-free moments as highlights of your day.

Ultimately, digital recharge provides you a chance to check in with yourself and discover more about who you are. They allow you to explore interests and hobbies that screen time might have overshadowed. Whether finding a new passion or rekindling old ones, these offline moments offer valuable insights into what makes you happy. By embracing the balance between online and offline worlds, you create space for personal growth and deeper connections with the people and activities that matter most to you.

Remember, taking control of your digital habits empowers you to live more intentionally and mindfully. The benefits are endless: improved focus, reduced stress, and enhanced well-being await those willing to unplug occasionally.

Using Social Media Positively

Social media can be a powerful learning and personal growth tool when used to its full potential. The internet is packed with awesome learning opportunities—whether you're into science, art, or what's happening around the world. There's so much knowledge out there, shared by experts and people who genuinely care about what they teach.

The digital age has given us the unique ability to explore deeper into fascinating subjects, learning from experts who are committed to sharing their wealth of knowledge. By thoughtfully choosing your social media feed to include an array of educational content, you are not merely enhancing your knowledge base but effectively broadening your horizon and inviting many new ideas and perspectives into your life. It's like possessing a massive library at your fingertips, ready to be explored whenever you desire.

By creating and sharing your own chosen content, you can further tap into social media's potential for positive influence. Sharing posts representing your values and goals allows you to contribute meaningfully to the digital community. Consider how the power of your words and images can inspire others.

Sharing personal triumphs and insights can motivate peers who are experiencing similar struggles. Remembering that each post holds the power to communicate who you genuinely are and what you fundamentally stand for is important. Being deliberate and thoughtful about your digital presence helps you build a supportive community bound by common values and shared interests.

Being a responsible digital citizen means treating others with respect, even when you disagree with them. Everyone comes from different backgrounds, and their life experiences shape how they see the world. It's important to keep things respectful and kind during online conversations. If you see someone being hurtful or spreading false information, don't just scroll past; report it. Standing up against cyberbullying and misinformation helps make social media a safer, more positive space where everyone can feel welcome.

As we conclude this chapter on navigating the digital landscape, remember that social media is what you choose to make of it. Using it with good judgment and intention makes it a powerful tool for empowerment, learning, and forming deep connections.

The next chapter will explore stress management strategies, equipping you with practical tools to enhance your mental resilience and emotional fortitude. Together, these skills will support your journey toward improving your self-esteem and thriving in today's hectic world.

Chapter 12

Long-Term Strategies for Self-Esteem

Building a Daily Routine for Self-Confidence

Imagine waking up each morning with purpose, refreshed and ready to tackle the day. Routines are essential for instilling confidence and stability in our often busy lives. Think of these routines as training that builds your strength and skills; they give you the foundation to show up strong and confident."

Make sure you make your bed. Your first accomplishment of the day.

Establishing a structured daily routine provides predictability and gives you a sense of control over your life. This consistency is vital for boosting mental clarity, reducing anxiety, and enhancing overall well-being (Clear Behavioral Health, n.d.).

Starting your day with confidence-boosting rituals can set the tone for successfully navigating challenges. For instance, a morning routine that includes stretching or light exercise can energize your body and mind. Some find that practicing positive affirmations in the mirror encourages self-assurance, while others prefer writing down their intentions for the day, focusing on what they hope to accomplish. These rituals might seem small, but their impact on your mindset and energy levels can be huge.

Consistency is crucial. Just as musicians practice daily to perfect their craft, maintaining a routine boosts your resolve and mental strength. This cultivates a stable environment where you feel secure and capable. Over time, these daily rituals become second nature, seamlessly adding mindfulness into your life and empowering you to face new experiences confidently.

Creating an empowering routine isn't about inflexible schedules but designing activities that improve your self-assurance. Consider incorporating positive affirmations into your daily practice, reminding yourself of your strengths and capabilities. Setting daily intentions can guide your actions and focus, providing direction and purpose. For example, choosing a theme or word for the day, such as "growth" or "kindness," can influence your interactions and decisions.

Incorporating self-care practices into your routine is equally essential. Self-care isn't a luxury; it's a necessity for maintaining confidence and mental well-being. Simple relaxation techniques like meditation or stretching can reduce stress and improve focus. Engaging in activities that nurture your physical health, such as regular exercise and mindful eating, significantly impacts how you perceive yourself. When you prioritize self-care, you tell yourself that you matter and deserve attention.

As the day winds down, reflecting on your achievements reinforces self-worth. Keeping a nightly journal of accomplishments and positive experiences encourages gratitude and self-awareness. This practice shifts focus from what went wrong to what went right, highlighting personal growth and progress. A brief reflective meditation before bed can help clear your mind, preparing you for restful sleep and another day of opportunities.

Reflection Section: Designing Your Daily Routine

Consider your current routine: What activities already boost your confidence? What could you add or change to enhance your self-assurance? Spend time brainstorming and writing down ideas for morning rituals, self-care practices, and evening reflections. Experiment with these over a week and notice any changes in how you feel about yourself.

Creating a daily routine is an ongoing process of tweaks and touch-ups. As life evolves, so should your routines, adapting to changing needs and priorities. Some days may require more flexibility, while others benefit from sticking to structure. Finding balance is ensuring your routine supports rather than limits you.

These strategies aren't about perfection; they're about progress. Embrace each day as an opportunity to build your confidence through intentional actions and choices. Over time, you'll find that your routine supports not just daily life but a lifelong journey toward self-discovery and empowerment.

The Role of Gratitude in Sustained Self-Esteem

Gratitude is a quiet yet powerful tool for enhancing self-esteem, offering a way to foster a more positive outlook. At its core, gratitude is the appreciation for what we have rather than what we don't. It's about recognizing the good around us, which can help build a more optimistic life view.

Psychology tells us that gratitude doesn't just feel good but improves mental health by making life feel lighter and more meaningful. When you practice gratitude, you create new pathways in your brain that enhance your well-being, making you more resilient in the face of challenges.

Consider stories of people who've turned their lives around through gratitude. Take Anna, who once felt constantly behind her peers and their accomplishments and was often stressed or anxious. But when she started practicing daily gratitude, she noticed a shift. Instead of focusing on what she didn't have, she cherished the small victories and simple joys, like a sunny day or a friend's smile. Her relationships improved, and her confidence grew as she realized how much she had to be thankful for.

Try keeping a gratitude journal to incorporate gratitude into your daily life. Journaling doesn't have to be fancy; a simple notebook will do. Each day, write down three things you're grateful for. They could be as significant as a major achievement or as small as enjoying your favorite meal. Over time, this practice can transform how you see the world, helping you focus more on all you have and cherish.

Sharing your gratitude with others also deepens its impact. Whether through thank-you notes or heartfelt conversations, expressing thanks can strengthen bonds and create a ripple effect of positivity.

Gratitude isn't just about feeling good; it affects your relationships. The simple act of expressing how thankful you are can improve friendships by promoting trust and understanding. In family settings, gratitude can shift dynamics from criticism to appreciation, encouraging everyone to focus on each other's strengths rather than shortcomings.

To practice gratitude within family dynamics, consider exercises like going around the dinner table each night and sharing one thing you're thankful for, encouraging open communication, and helping family members recognize the support they offer each other. Even small gestures like leaving a note of thanks to a parent or sibling can be a game-changer.

Visualization exercises can help you grow a deeper sense of gratitude. Imagine yourself surrounded by everything you need: love, support, and resources, and let that feeling fill you up. Reflective prompts can also guide you in recognizing life's blessings. Ask yourself questions like "What went well today?" or "What do I appreciate about myself?" These reflections encourage you to see the glass as half full rather than half empty.

Gratitude is more than just a feeling; it's a practice that can transform your life if you let it. It encourages you to slow down and savor the present moment, appreciating what you have rather than constantly seeking more. By integrating gratitude into your routine, you can care for your self-esteem and encourage a mindset that appreciates the full spectrum of what life offers.

Incorporating gratitude into your everyday life might seem simple, but it greatly benefits your mental health and personal growth. As you continue this practice, your self-esteem strengthens as you become more in tune with the positive aspects of your life. Gratitude helps transform ordinary moments into extraordinary ones by highlighting the beauty all around you. Even in challenging times, gratitude can serve as a guiding light, helping you navigate difficulties with grace and resilience.

Accountability Buddies: Stronger Together

Imagine having someone by your side who not only shares your goals but also energetically nudges you forward during moments of self-doubt or when you're feeling stuck. That's the power of having an accountability buddy.

This person doesn't just play the role of a cheerleader; they can be a crucial ally in your ongoing quest for self-improvement and the development of your self-esteem. Together, you forge a strong support system where mutual encouragement fuels progress.

When you pursue your goals alongside someone else, the path appears less overwhelming. The shared experience eases the journey and creates a bond that builds enduring trust and resilience. You might have different objectives, yet the shared commitment to growth significantly strengthens both of you. Successful partnerships like these have been the backbone of countless achievements, from personal fitness milestones to academic triumphs and professional successes.

In choosing an accountability buddy who best complements your journey, looking for someone whose values and long-term goals align with yours is vital. This alignment ensures you're both on the same page, making collaboration smooth and seamless. Your buddy must be reliable, genuine, and wholeheartedly invested in your success.

Clear communication serves as the key to nurturing and maintaining this relationship. By establishing expectations early, you can prevent misunderstandings from surfacing later on. It's wise to decide together how often you'll check in, whether through weekly phone calls or frequent text updates. These conversations are important, as they keep you both accountable and motivated.

Regular check-ins provide a safe space to celebrate wins, openly discuss setbacks, and strategically plan the next steps. The consistency of these interactions reinforces your commitment to your goals. Knowing someone is counting on you significantly boosts your motivation to follow through. Whether you choose structured meetings or laid-back, casual catch-ups, ensure these interactions are constructive, focused on progress, and always positive.

Working collaboratively with your buddy can transform challenges into golden opportunities for growth. When you face obstacles, brainstorming solutions can lead to creative breakthroughs. Establishing mutual goals encourages you to push each other toward success.

You might practice role-playing scenarios to imagine potential challenges and develop strategies to overcome them. This teamwork enhances problem-solving skills and deepens the partnership, creating a sense of shared accomplishment and achievement.

Picture yourself navigating a particularly tricky situation with your partner's support, transforming what once seemed impossible into a manageable task. Their perspective might reveal solutions you hadn't considered, expanding your toolkit for handling future challenges with greater confidence. The collective wisdom of two minds working together is a powerful force.

This relationship becomes a cherished, safe space where you can confidently be vulnerable about your fears, hopes, and dreams without judgment. In this supportive dynamic, self-esteem soars as you witness your growth and celebrate each other's successes.

You learn to genuinely appreciate the journey as much as the destination, embracing the understanding that growth is an ongoing and ever-evolving process. The partnership reinforces the idea that we're stronger together than alone, proving that support can come from unexpected places and deliver incredible rewards.

In this partnership, every small victory is magnified, contributing to a greater sense of achievement and self-worth. As you continue working with your accountability buddy, you'll inevitably discover new strengths within yourself and deepen your understanding of what it means to strive for personal excellence alongside someone who truly shares your vision.

Ultimately, the journey with an accountability buddy is about far more than just reaching goals; it's about building a solid foundation of resilience, an unbreakable connection, and unwavering self-belief. Through shared experiences and mutual support, you unlock new dimensions of potential within yourself, all while strengthening the bond that empowers both partners to rise above challenges and embrace their authentic selves.

Sustaining Growth: Adapting to Life's Changes

Change is as inevitable as the sunrise, and while it can sometimes feel overwhelming, it's a powerful turning point for growth. Life is full of twists and turns, each offering a fresh perspective and unique lessons. Whether it's moving to a new city, starting at a different school, or even welcoming a new family member, these changes, though potentially challenging, present exceptional opportunities for personal development and expansion of the mind.

Sam moved across the country during his sophomore year. At first, the transition filled him with uncertainty.. However, it ultimately served to push him past his comfort zone. He embraced new friendships and dove into unexplored hobbies and teams, revealing abilities and interests that he wasn't aware he had.

Navigating change requires a dynamic blend of flexibility and resilience, like the transformative journey of a caterpillar into a butterfly. It's about building the proper mindset necessary to embrace uncertainty, viewing it not simply as a hurdle to cross but as an important chance to learn and grow from facing the unknown.

Mindset exercises, such as visualizing yourself managing new situations and focusing your mind on feelings of confidence and capability, serve as mental preparation for when life hits you with the unexpected. This kind of mental rehearsal doesn't just prepare you for unavoidable challenges but allows you to approach them with openness and determination, transforming fear into proactive courage.

Balance during transitions acts as a steadying anchor in the storm. By grounding yourself in routines that provide stability yet remain adjustable, you build a flexible environment that encourages growth. While giving a comforting framework, routines should also accommodate the necessary changes to adapt to new situations.

Personal growth is a lifelong process, a journey that thrives on curiosity and continuous exploration. Setting personal growth goals, thoughtfully tailored to fit various life stages, keeps you marching forward purposefully. Whether diving into the complexities of a new language, practicing a skill, or searching for new and different hobbies, each serves as a stepping stone toward a more enriched life experience.

Engaging in activities you've never tried before broadens your skill set and strengthens your mental capabilities, keeping your mind sharp and adaptable. You might stumble upon hidden talents or passions that provide joy and fulfillment, making your life shine even brighter.

Performing regular check-ins with yourself ensures you remain on a path aligned with your hopes and dreams. Take time to reassess achievements and challenges you've faced along your journey. This process is about understanding your experiences to guide future actions.

The beauty of life lies in its unpredictability, and learning to adapt to change is a valuable skill that enhances self-esteem and boosts confidence. Embracing change with a positive attitude does more than help you navigate challenges; it propels you toward new possibilities for personal development. As you continue your growth journey, remember that each experience, whether planned or unexpected, contributes to your journey of self-discovery.

Life is about adapting and growing with each experience we encounter. By embracing change with resilience, establishing personal goals, and reflecting on your progress, you lay a foundation for sustained self-esteem and personal fulfillment.

Consider how your adaptability enhances your connections with others. Building strong relationships demands flexibility and understanding, qualities honed through personal growth and self-awareness.

Conclusion

As we come to the end of this journey together, let's take a moment to reflect on the path we've traveled. We've explored essential themes to help you build self-esteem, develop a strong self-image, and enhance mental resilience. Throughout this book, we've dug into strategies that empower you to understand and embrace who you are, building a genuine sense of confidence to withstand life's challenges.

The core of our discussions revolved around self-awareness and emotional intelligence. We've seen how vital it is to become in tune with your thoughts and emotions to understand yourself better and connect more deeply with others. Resilience has been a recurring theme, emphasizing the importance of bouncing back from setbacks with determination and grace. We've also touched on mindfulness and how being present in the moment can significantly influence your self-perception and interactions.

Social skills were another key focus, as they play a crucial role in making meaningful connections. By practicing effective communication and learning to read social cues, you can navigate social situations with ease and confidence. These skills open doors to forming supportive networks, which are crucial in your growth journey.

Remember, building self-esteem is not a destination but a lifelong journey. It's about understanding your unique qualities, embracing individuality, and striving for personal growth. Every step you take in this direction adds to your strength and resilience. It's important to recognize that this journey is uniquely yours, and taking it at your own pace is okay.

Now, it's time to put these insights into practice. Real change happens when you actively apply the strategies and exercises we've discussed. Whether setting achievable goals with the S.M.A.R.T. framework, practicing gratitude daily, or engaging in positive self-talk, choose one strategy to focus on right now. This practical application will lead to real-life improvements in your self-esteem and confidence.

As you travel this path, remember that challenges are a natural part of life. They don't define you; your response to them does. You have the tools to overcome obstacles and thrive. Trust in your ability to grow and adapt through each experience. You are capable, and you are strong.

A crucial component of this journey is the support system you build around you. Friends, family, and mentors are your allies. Don't hesitate to reach out to them for guidance and encouragement. Their support can provide the perspective and reassurance you need, especially during tough times.

Take time to reflect on your progress regularly. Celebrate your achievements, no matter how small they may seem. Each victory is a testament to your growth and determination. Reflection helps you acknowledge your progress and reinforces your commitment to self-discovery.

Change will happen no matter what, and being flexible is key to maintaining self-esteem. Embrace change as an opportunity for growth. Each transition, big or small, teaches lessons that contribute to your resilience and confidence. Be open to these lessons and let them guide you.

On a personal note, I want you to know how much I believe in your potential. Over the years, I've witnessed countless young individuals transform into confident, resilient beings. I do not doubt that you can achieve this. Your journey is just beginning, and the possibilities are endless. Remember, you are not alone. I am here, cheering you on every step of the way.

Confidence Over Fear

Thank you for letting me be part of your journey. Now, go out there and shine. You've got this.

S.M.A.R.T. Goals Worksheet

Set a goal that works for YOU! A great goal is S.M.A.R.T.

S: Specific: What exactly do you want to accomplish? Be clear and detailed.

M:Measurable: How will you know when you've reached your goal? What can you track?

A: Achievable: Is your goal realistic? Do you have the resources and time to do it?

R: Relevant: Why is this goal important to you? How does it connect to your bigger dreams?

T: Time-Bound: When will you achieve this goal? Set a deadline!

Final S.M.A.R.T. Goal Statement:

Put it all together in one powerful sentence:
By the deadline, I'll achieve (specific goal) through (steps you'll take), and I'll know I'm successful when (how you'll measure it).

Example (for inspiration!):

My goal is to improve my grades in math.

S: I want to raise my math grade from a C to a B.

M: I'll track my quiz and test scores.

A: I'll study for 30 extra minutes each day and meet with my teacher once a week.

R: It's important because I want to prepare for high school honors math.

T: I want to reach this goal by the end of the semester.

Final Statement: *By November 1st, I'll raise my math grade from a C to a B by studying 30 extra minutes daily and meeting with my teacher weekly. I'll know I've succeeded when my report card shows a B or higher.*

🏀 Keeping the Game Alive

Share What You've Learned. Help Someone Else Win.

"When we lift each other, we all rise."

— Coach Mary

You did it! You've reached the end of the book—and that's a big win. You've learned tools to build self-esteem, face challenging moments, and believe in the amazing person you are becoming.

Now, would you help someone else start their journey?

By leaving a quick review on Amazon, you're showing other teens, parents, teachers, and counselors where they can find the help they've been searching for. Your honest words can make a real difference.

Imagine your review helping someone:

Find their confidence again.

Get through a hard day.

Discover they're not alone.

Believe that change is possible.

You're passing the ball. You're keeping the game alive.

Self-esteem grows when we support each other. Your review keeps that growth going for the next person who needs it.

Click or scan the link to leave your review: https://www.

amazon.com/review/review-your-purchases/?asin=
B0F9XHRBB9

Thank you for being here. Thank you for being *you*.

With heart and high fives,

Coach Mary Rossignol

"Start right here, one page at a time."

Circle Back & Pay It Forward

You've reached the final page, but this isn't the end. In fact, it's a powerful new beginning.

Now that you've grown, learned, and stretched your mindset, go back to **Chapter 1**. You're no longer the same person who first opened this book. You'll see things differently. Feel more. Understand deeper. Each page will speak to you in a new way, because *you've changed.*

But don't keep this journey to yourself.

Invite **three friends** to walk this path with you. Grow together. Support one another. Share your wins and setbacks, because transformation sticks when it's shared.

Let's do the math: if it takes each person just **30 days** to read this book and pass it on to **three more people**, the ripple spreads fast. In less than a **year**, your impact could reach over **1,000 people**. However, if this trend continues for four **years**, the number skyrockets. You could be part of a chain reaction that reaches **over 10 million lives**.

That's the magic of the **six degrees of separation**—you're only six people away from anyone in the world. And right now, you're one powerful choice away from starting a movement that can change lives across schools, cities, and even countries.

So go back. Begin again. And this time, bring others with you.

One act of kindness can change someone's day or life.

About the Author

Coach Mary Rossignol brings over 40 years of coaching and mentoring experience to teens, having worked with both boys and girls across public schools, private academies, and competitive club teams. A lifelong athlete, passionate educator, and spiritual servant leader, Mary is committed to helping young people become the best version of themselves, on and off the court.

Raised as the youngest of five, with four loving, athletic brothers who excelled in sports, life, and business, Mary was the answer to her mother Flo's prayers. After four boys, Florence vowed to name her next child Mary if she was blessed with a daughter. Five years later, that promise was fulfilled.

Proudly 100% Italian American, Mary's grandparents on both sides immigrated through Staten Island, New York. Her strong family roots, deep faith in God and Jesus, and unwavering commitment to servant leadership have shaped her life's purpose.

Mary's accomplishments are exceptional. A decorated All-American in basketball and softball, she was inducted into the Lakewood Hall of Fame in Southern California and won multiple California Interscholastic Federation (CIF) championships as both a student-athlete and coach. She received the Brian Piccolo Amateur Athlete of the Year Award, joining John

Cappelletti, who earned the professional version of the same honor that year.

As Head Girls' Basketball Coach at JSerra Catholic High School in Southern California, Mary has led her team to over 200 career wins. JSerra competes in the Trinity League, one of the nation's most competitive high school sports leagues. Inspired early on by her brother Pete, an NCAA Division I softball coach with over 900 career wins and multiple College World Series appearances, Mary knew she was born to lead and mentor.

She has guided 26 student-athletes to collegiate-level sports, with her coaching legacy defined by life skills, discipline, a strong work ethic, and mental toughness. She emphasizes building character, fostering mutual respect, and helping teens realize their full potential.

Mary is deeply grateful for her family, friends, and faith. A lifelong learner, fierce competitor, and devoted wife, she has been married to Tony for over 30 years. Together, they continue to inspire, encourage, and uplift the next generation, **"One page at a time."**

References

- *Self-esteem - APA Dictionary of Psychology* https://dictionary.apa.org/self-esteem
- *Self-Esteem Development From Age 14 to 30 Years* https://www.apa.org/pubs/journals/releases/psp-101-3-607.pdf
- *The role of self-esteem in the development of psychiatric ...* https://pmc.ncbi.nlm.nih.gov/articles/PMC5747942/
- *Self-esteem and self-confidence - University of Queensland* https://my.uq.edu.au/information-and-services/student-support/health-and-wellbeing/self-help-resources/self-esteem-and-self-confidence
- *How Authenticity Can Transform Your Life and Happiness* https://www.randytaran.com/blog/how-authenticity-can-transform-your-life-and-happiness
- *Understanding Teenage Mental Health: Navigating Social ...* https://behavioralwellnessgroup.com/understanding-teenage-mental-health-navigating-social-pressures/
- *Creative Self-Expression for Health, Coping, and Resilience* https://www.psychologytoday.com/us/blog/going-beyond-intelligence/201909/creative-self-expression-health-coping-and-resilience
- *How to Build Your Personal Brand in High School* https://summer.harvard.edu/blog/prepare-for-college/how-to-build-your-personal-brand-in-high-school/
- *Resilience and mental health in children and adolescents* https://pmc.ncbi.nlm.nih.gov/articles/PMC8500371/
- *31 Famous Individuals Who Overcame Huge Setbacks* https://www.becomedamngood.com/post/the-ideal-mindset-14-famous-individuals-who-overcame-huge-setbacks
- *Boosting Mental Toughness in Young Athletes & 20 ...* https://positivepsychology.com/mental-toughness-for-young-athletes/
- *How to Build a Teen's Emotional Regulation Skills* https://www.spokaneimagine.com/mental-health-blog/emotional-regulation-skills-for-teens-and-how-to-develop-them/
- *Feedback vs Criticism: A Manager's Guide to Constructive ...* https://www.coffeepals.com/blog/feedback-vs-criticism-a-managers-guide-to-constructive-communication#
- *Peer Pressure (for Teens) | Nemours KidsHealth* https://kidshealth.org/en/teens/peer-pressure.html

- *15 Tips to Build Self-Esteem and Confidence in Teens* https://biglifejournal.com/blogs/blog/build-self-esteem-confidence-teens?srsltid=AfmBOorSC5ydGm70jg808aNgdB5lAY5wOaA9dXjbaSsDbq1AaTyVZxmJ
- *Social Media and Youth Mental Health* https://www.hhs.gov/surgeongeneral/reports-and-publications/youth-mental-health/social-media/index.html
- *Adolescent Family Context and Adult Identity Formation* https://pmc.ncbi.nlm.nih.gov/articles/PMC2806681/
- *Supporting effective communication in your teenager* https://parents.au.reachout.com/parenting-skills/effective-communication/effective-communication-and-teenagers
- *How Toxic Relationships Affect Teens' Mental Health* https://blumebh.com/resources/how-toxic-friendships-and-relationships-affect-teenagers-mental-health/
- *Building Resilience in Adolescents* https://www.alisbh.com/blog/building-resilience-in-adolescents/
- *Lessons from Famous Failures: What They Teach Us About ...* https://vocal.media/motivation/lessons-from-famous-failures-what-they-teach-us-about-success
- *Resilience to emotional distress in response to failure ...* https://www.sciencedirect.com/science/article/abs/pii/S0272735816302902
- *Growth Mindset vs. Fixed Mindset: What's the Difference?* https://online.hbs.edu/blog/post/growth-mindset-vs-fixed-mindset
- *Building Student Resilience Toolkit* https://safesupportivelearning.ed.gov/building-student-resilience-toolkit
- *Teen Stress: 10 Stress-Management Skills for Teenagers* https://www.newportacademy.com/resources/mental-health/teen-stress-relief/
- *Powerful Relaxation Skills for Teens Today | Newport Academy* https://www.newportacademy.com/resources/well-being/relaxation-skills-for-teens
- *Creative Arts: Enhancing Mental Health and Well-being* https://www.psychiatry.org/news-room/apa-blogs/creative-arts-enhancing-mental-health
- *For Teens: Creating Your Personal Stress-Management Plan* https://www.healthychildren.org/English/healthy-living/emotional-wellness/Building-Resilience/Pages/For-Teens-Creating-Your-Personal-Stress-Management-Plan.aspx

- *How to write SMART goals (with examples)* https://www.atlassian.com/blog/productivity/how-to-write-smart-goals
- *From Small Steps to Big Wins: The Importance of Celebrating* https://www.psychologytoday.com/us/blog/empower-your-mind/202406/from-small-steps-to-big-wins-the-importance-of-celebrating
- *8 Ways to Help Your Teen Stop Procrastinating* https://www.psychologytoday.com/us/blog/promoting-empathy-your-teen/202210/8-ways-help-your-teen-stop-procrastinating
- *Doing What Matters - The Power of Values-Based Living* https://momentumpsychology.com/doing-what-matters-the-power-of-values-based-living/
- *12 Benefits of Time Management for Teens* https://weekplan.net/12-benefits-of-time-management-for-teens
- *The Eisenhower Matrix: Introduction & 3-Minute Video Tutorial* https://www.eisenhower.me/eisenhower-matrix/
- *Top 5 Free Apps for Students: Time Management* ... https://reclaim.ai/blog/student-time-management-app
- *Impact of Extracurricular Activities on Students by Nikki* ... https://www2.uwstout.edu/content/lib/thesis/2009/2009wilsonn.pdf
- *Tips for Teens: Building Healthy Communication Skills* https://www.thrivetrainingconsulting.com/tips-for-teens-building-healthy-communication-skills/
- *Understanding Different Types of Social Cues* https://www.verywellhealth.com/social-cues-5204407
- *Healthy Friendships in Adolescence* https://www.chconline.org/resourcelibrary/healthy-friendships-in-adolescence/
- *Developing Effective Group Communication Skills in High* ... https://everydayspeech.com/blog-posts/general/developing-effective-group-communication-skills-in-high-school-students/
- *How Using Social Media Affects Teenagers* https://childmind.org/article/how-using-social-media-affects-teenagers/
- *Current perspectives: the impact of cyberbullying on* ... https://pmc.ncbi.nlm.nih.gov/articles/PMC4126576/
- *The Power of Digital Detox* https://www.nkch.org/blog/the-power-of-digital-detox
- *Tips to Help Teens Stay Safe and Healthy Using Social* ... https://jedfoundation.org/tips-to-help-teens-stay-safe-and-healthy-on-social-media/
- *Routines for Teens | Clear Behavioral Health* https://clearbehavioralhealth.com/importance-of-implementing-routines

- *13 Most Popular Gratitude Exercises & Activities* https://positivepsychology.com/gratitude-exercises/
- *Accountability Partners: Don't Achieve Your Goals Alone!* https://recreation.duke.edu/story/accountability-partners-dont-achieve-your-goals-alone/
- *Learn How Adaptation Is a Key to Embracing Change and ...* https://www.psychologytoday.com/us/blog/sustainable-life-satisfaction/202009/learn-how-adaptation-is-key-embracing-change-and-growth
- *AI Generated Art | Fotor Photo Editor* https://www.fotor.com/images/create

Made in the USA
Columbia, SC
21 June 2025

a6c35144-2a85-44ce-accc-6ea83554a8c6R01